The Past in Prehistoric Socie

The idea of prehistory dates from the nineteenth century and sometimes seems to be a relic of the colonial era, but Richard Bradley contends that it is still a vital area for research. His claim is based on the argument that it was only through a combination of oral tradition and the experience of encountering ancient material culture that people were able to formulate a sense of their own pasts without written records. In effect, they were forced to become archaeologists themselves.

The Past in Prehistoric Societies applies this argument to the archaeology of Europe, presenting a series of case studies which extend from the Palaeolithic period to the early Middle Ages and from the Alps to Scandinavia. It first examines how archaeologists might study origin myths and develops into an account of the different ways in which prehistoric people would have inherited artefacts, settlements and even whole landscapes from the past. It discusses the claim that monuments were built to contrive the memories of later generations and also investigates the ways in which ancient remains might have been invested with new meanings long after their original significance had been forgotten. Finally, the author compares the procedures of current excavation and field survey in the light of these examples.

It has only been in recent years that archaeologists have studied what has become known as 'the past in the past' and this work explores the potential for new research in this area both in the field and in the museum. In order to convey that message to a wide professional and amateur audience, the work includes a large number of detailed case studies, is fully illustrated and has been written in an extremely accessible style.

Richard Bradley is Professor of Archaeology at Reading University. His main interests are in European prehistory, social archaeology and landscape. Among his recent books are *An Archaeology of Natural Places*, *The Significance of Monuments* and *Rock Art and the Prehistory of Atlantic Europe*, all published by Routledge.

The Past in Prehistoric Societies

Richard Bradley

London and New York

First published 2002
by Routledge
11 New Fetter Lane, London EC4P 4EE

Simultaneously published in the USA and Canada
by Routledge
29 West 35th Street, New York, NY 10001

Routledge is an imprint of the Taylor & Francis Group

Typeset in Baskerville by
BOOK NOW Ltd
Printed and bound in Great Britain by
Biddles Ltd, Guildford and King's Lynn

British Library Cataloguing in Publication Data
A catalogue record for this book is available
from the British Library

Library of Congress Cataloging in Publication Data
A catalog record for this book has been requested

ISBN 0-415-27627-6 (hbk)
ISBN 0-415-27628-4 (pbk)

For Andy, Hannah and Lise

Contents

Figures

Tables

Preface

This is a book that I have been wanting to write for a long time. The first steps were taken in articles which appeared between 10 and 15 years ago, and I had the chance to explore some of the same issues in two edited volumes of the journal *World Archaeology*. The first appeared in 1993 with the title 'Conceptions of Time and Ancient Society', while a second, co-edited with Howard Williams, came out in 1998 and was concerned with 'The Reuse of Ancient Monuments'. I employed some of the same ideas during my own fieldwork in Britain, Portugal and Spain.

Why has this book been so long in the making? There are perhaps two reasons for this. The first was a certain unease at the way in which time and memory had been discussed by prehistorians. It had been hard to bring their abstractions down to earth and harder still to relate these ideas to the material world. The second reason for delay was the sheer mass of material that deserved to be considered. That was only possible because I had a period of research leave from Reading University and access to an excellent library in Oxford. Even though this account uses only a fraction of the literature I consulted, the entire undertaking would have been unthinkable without a prolonged period of exposure to unfamiliar sources.

I have been greatly helped in this task by four people: by John Creighton, Martin Henig and Andy Jones, who have read the text in draft and offered many comments on its approach, contents and style, and by Aaron Watson who is responsible for the illustrations.

I completed this book after I returned from fieldwork in Norway conducted together with Andy Jones, Hannah Sackett and Lise Nordenborg Myhre. It was a wonderfully creative time and it brought me back to my unfinished text with new enthusiasm. The dedication is my way of thanking them.

Richard Bradley

Chapter 1

Introduction

Darwin's Christmas dinner

At Port Desire

There is a story which sums up the development of prehistoric archaeology.

In 1833, the Admiralty survey ship, *The Beagle*, was moored off Port Desire on the coast of Patagonia. It was here that its most famous passenger, Charles Darwin, sat down to his Christmas dinner. If the occasion was traditional, the menu certainly was not, for much of the food eaten on the voyage had to be of local origin. In this case it included a kind of ostrich which he himself had shot. At the end of the meal, the bird had been reduced to its head, its legs and a wing. It was at this point that Darwin realised that he had just eaten a new species. The leftovers were collected together and documented for their return to England, where the remains of his dinner were enshrined in the scientific definition of *Rhea Darwinii* (Desmond and Moore 1991: 144–5 and 225).

Darwin's experience was rather like that of the field archaeologist, for his work was based on material evidence. During the early nineteenth century natural history could be a destructive business. Before the adoption of photography, the best ways of describing animals were by trapping or shooting them (Barber 1980). They could be classified, illustrated and discussed, but in many cases this was only possible because these creatures had been killed. In time, photographs were to provide another medium for capturing their appearance and for recording their behaviour in the wild. Darwin's fieldwork had its counterpart in archaeological excavation which also involved the elimination of the very phenomena that it set out to record, but it is hard to see how it could have been otherwise. We may find it troubling that Darwin should have combined hunting with natural history, but he would have achieved much less if he had used other methods of collecting information. In the same way, an archaeology based entirely on surface remains would have been quite incapable of coming to terms with the complexity of its source material.

The comparison between archaeology and Darwin's field research has other aspects, too. Like the study of history, both involve the preservation of memories. A full description of the rhea would involve the appearance of the bird before it was cooked, just as the features revealed by excavation must be recorded before they are disturbed. The dead animals on which such pioneering studies depended have much in common with the extinct objects recovered by digging. The creatures were reanimated from lifeless corpses into vivid pictures and from field notes into documents, just as the remains on Darwin's dinner plate had to be studied and described before they could take their place in the scientific literature. These published accounts preserved the memory of discoveries that were already receding into the past. It was those texts that provided the basis for more ambitious interpretations.

The same was true of nineteenth century archaeology, for it was during this period that it began to change from an essentially literary pursuit into a more empirical discipline. For centuries, interpretations of the remote past had been built around written accounts, from the Bible to the works of the earliest historians. In Europe this meant that the sequence did not extend much further back than the Classical period, with the result that a disproportionate number of ancient monuments were attributed to the Greeks or Romans and their enemies. That perspective changed quite slowly because of the difficulties of building a chronology for earlier periods (Trigger 1989: chapters 2 and 3). On the other hand, the growing contacts between excavators and researchers in the sciences, including Darwin himself, resulted in the observations made in fieldwork gaining a new legitimacy. That development is marked by a greater concern with record-keeping. There was a gradual realisation that description and documentation were as much a part of archaeology as the use of literary evidence, and that is why some of the major monographs published at that time can still be used as a source of information today. It is important to understand the authors' original intentions, but, as secondary sources describing observations which could never be repeated, these studies ran in parallel with other records of scientific work; and, like them, they preserved the memory of information that might otherwise have been forgotten.

In their published form the texts produced by archaeologists became historical documents themselves, subject to the same kinds of scrutiny as other writings originating in the past. They also influenced conduct in the future, for they provided some of the materials through which later generations would come to terms with antiquities. These sources contribute to the presentation of what has become known as the 'heritage', but they do so at one remove, for, unlike historical documents, such accounts are not the raw material on which interpretations are based but simply a series of descriptions of past encounters with that evidence. Even with this limitation, they contribute to a form of memory that is intended to serve a wider audience. Indeed, collective memories of this kind play such a large role in contemporary politics that it is increasingly difficult for archaeological fieldwork to dispel the myths that become established.

One obvious example of such a myth is the existence of an ancient Celtic nation (Chapman, M. 1992). This has been important in Brittany where the great megalithic tombs of the Neolithic period were once interpreted as the work of the Veneti, who mounted such sustained resistance to Caesar. That myth, which was important in the growth of Breton nationalism, has been rejected by prehistorians, and yet it survives in popular belief in the exploits of Asterix. A similar kind of memory contributed to Darwin's experience off Port Desire. Why did he eat the rhea as part of a formal meal? On one level, Darwin was following the tradition of the Christmas dinner. On another, he was celebrating the origin of Christianity, a system of belief whose very significance his later work would do much to undermine. Christmas was one of its main festivals, and the sequence of rituals in the ecclesiastical calendar traced the course of a narrative that had been repeated for nearly 2000 years.

Two millennia were of little account in Darwin's research. His observations in South America did much to influence his view of natural selection. The rheas he had encountered in Patagonia played a small part in the theory of evolution, but the outcome of his investigation was fundamental, for it led him to conclude that human beings had originated at a much earlier date than had been implied in established sources, including the Bible. His thesis was unwelcome to the clergy, but even among his own followers it necessitated a new approach to the past. It enabled people to investigate human antiquity in a way that had been literally unthinkable when it seemed as if our species was created fully formed. It may be no accident that it was while Darwin was working towards these conclusions that the word 'prehistory' was invented (Chippindale 1988).

About prehistory

Prehistory is a term that can give rise to problems, although many of these stem from the ways in which the concept was applied in the nineteenth century. Taken literally, the word relates to the investigation of societies that do not have records or other written sources. They are *pre*historic because they cannot be studied by the methods of historians. In Continental usage this has been complicated by the use of another term, *protohistory*, to refer to the time in which communities without written testimony of their own existed concurrently with societies that did have documents; generally speaking, that was in the first millennium BC (Hawkes 1950). For the purposes of this account, I shall adhere to the simpler scheme.

Unfortunately, the word *prehistory* has not been used consistently because of the way in which archaeology and ethnography overlapped in Victorian thought. In 1865, Sir John Lubbock published his famous book *Pre-historic Times*. Its full title is rarely quoted: 'Pre-historic Times, as Illustrated by Ancient Remains *and the Manners and Customs of Modern Savages*' [my emphasis]. In keeping with that scheme, the section on 'The antiquity of man' leads into three others concerned with living communities. Among the topics considered are: 'Progress among savages', 'Skilfulness of savages', 'Ideas of decency', 'Curious customs', 'Low ideas of the deity', 'Moral and intellectual inferiority of savages', 'General wretchedness of savages' and, rather oddly, 'Neatness in sewing'. These follow a lengthy discussion of the archaeological sequence in selected areas of the Old and New Worlds, and the implication is clear. Even during the nineteenth century, there were communities whose ways of life were directly comparable with those of *prehistoric* peoples (Figure 1.1). These were the groups who had been left behind in the course of social evolution and for the most part they were also the ones who had to be educated in the ways of civilisation. Again that notion was influenced by the work of Darwin, although it was actually Herbert Spencer who extended the principles of natural selection to the study of human society (Trigger 1989: 93). By now the very idea of prehistory had taken on pejorative connotations.

Although that kind of conjectural history is no longer fashionable, it has had a longer currency than is sometimes supposed, for its approach is not all that different from the fashion for cross-cultural analysis that was such a feature of processual archaeology during the 1960s and 70s. This combined prehistory with the ethnographic present in a similar but more disciplined manner. Since then there has been a reaction. Trigger (1980) has complained about the tendency of his colleagues to treat the indigenous populations of North America as laboratory specimens, and Fabian's book, *Time and the Other*, showed how anthropologists could equate geographical remoteness with antiquity, so that non-Western societies might be thought of as existing in a past (Fabian 1983).

In fact the word *prehistory* has been used in two quite different ways. So far this account has concentrated on the first of these and has discussed what is really a particular sub-discipline within archaeology. It refers to the research of a number of specialists and the assumptions that they bring to their task. The term can be used in another way which is less vulnerable to political abuse. *Prehistory* is not simply a synonym for the uncivilised or remote, it also describes a particular

Figure 1.1 An Indian stone circle compared by Sir John Lubbock with prehistoric monuments in Europe.

Source: from Lubbock (1870).

conception of time. The distinction is akin to that found in social anthropology where what were once called 'primitive' societies are now described as 'traditional'.

The difficulty with this new terminology is that it could easily misrepresent the nature of archaeological analysis. It may be true that particular communities were governed by oral lore, but if their conduct was guided entirely by unwritten traditions, they are not among the sources that can be studied by prehistorians, whose only evidence is that of material remains. If archaeologists are to engage with such people at all, it will be because their material culture can be treated in similar ways to the texts produced by other communities. If past societies are to be described as 'traditional', it must be because their artefacts, buildings and landscapes provide evidence for such traditions. Otherwise there is a risk of substituting one unsatisfactory term for another.

Telling the time

Traditions can only develop through the passage of time, and time, we might suppose, is the archaeologist's medium. But it is generally taken for granted, and this leaves some important questions unanswered. Prehistorians have only recently considered this subject. Time, they claim, must not be treated separately from social life, for it is culturally constructed and must be understood in terms of local practices. Times are multiple and overlapping; there is no single strand to be followed from the past to the future. Gosden puts this point particularly well:

> All action is timed action, which uses the imprint of the past to create an anticipation of the future. Together the body and material things form the flow of the past into the future. Human time flows on a number of levels. Each level represents a different aspect of the framework of reference. Long-term frames of reference are those within which we are socialised, made up of the particular shape of the landscape, historically special sets of relations between people and definite forms of interaction between people and the world. . . . Long-term systems of reference are contained within the shape of the cultural landscape. . . . Within this larger structure . . . are contained the more point-specific sorts of evidence deriving from short-term and specific acts.
>
> (Gosden 1994: 17–18)

Time is part of the process of living in society. Just as no two societies are the same, there are many different ways in which time may be experienced and described.

In fact it may be only in modern industrial society that people measure time according to a single scale. That is because, under capitalism, time costs money. It is a feature which involves specific expenditure and can be portioned out like any other commodity that carries a financial value (Shanks and Tilley 1987:

chapter 5). But in other contexts time may be experienced quite differently. It can be conceived according to many different scales. For instance, it may be related to the sequence of natural phenomena, like the lunar month and the annual cycle of the seasons. It may also refer to the passage of human generations, so that it is calibrated by the important events that punctuate the lives of individual people, like birth, initiation, maturity and death (Adam 1990; Gell 1992; Hughes and Trautman 1995). The possibilities are limitless.

If time can be experienced in different ways, even within the same society, it can also be studied at a number of different scales. One scheme was devised by the French historian, Braudel, who distinguished between the rapidly changing *history of events*, the *medium term* of economic cycles, and what he called the *longue durée* which relates mainly to demography and the natural environment (Braudel 1969). Each of these is reflected in an academic division of labour, so that political history is mainly concerned with the first of these time scales and economic history with the medium term. The *longue durée* has more influence on landscape history. It is a matter of choice which scale is most appropriate to the subject being studied. Gosden (1994) suggests that a similar division can be made in prehistoric archaeology, and he distinguishes between the day-to-day activities of people in the past, which were governed by *habit*, and the long term continuities expressed by monuments and similar structures which provide evidence of *public time*. It is one of the tasks of archaeologists to consider how these were related to one another in particular situations in the past.

If time is a social construction and can be conceptualised in so many different ways, how can it be studied by archaeologists? I find Gell's book, *The Anthropology of Time*, especially helpful here. Gell (1992) distinguishes between two fundamentally different ways of thinking about time. Following earlier writers, he distinguishes between what he calls the A-series and the B-series. In the A-series, time is conceived in terms of three states – past, present and future – while the B-series distinguishes between events which exist 'before' or 'after' any particular moment.

The A-series is the subjective time experienced by human actors. As we have seen, there are numerous ways in which time is reckoned in non-Western societies and it is quite clear that the notion of an unbroken chain of events reaching into an infinite future is a peculiarly local way of perceiving duration, even if it is one to which modern industrial societies subscribe. In fact, time may be considered according to many different schemes, all of which fall within the A-series, and it is perfectly possible for it to be experienced on more than one level within the same society, according to the contexts in which it is most significant. In the same way, time can be experienced quite differently between the people in neighbouring communities. It follows that it is most unlikely that prehistoric groups experienced the passage of time in exactly the same ways as we do today. Their responses are likely to have been so varied that it will be difficult to interpret them now.

The B-series, on the other hand, plays a fundamental role in the sciences. It is universal and provides the basic measure to which all other schemes are related. Yet in Gell's thesis the A-series and B-series are not alternatives to one another. Rather, the B-series describes a universal process on which 'subjective time' offers a commentary. Both kinds of time scheme need to be considered, but it is essential to retain some hold on 'scientific time' for it provides a common measure according to which other systems can be compared.

This scheme has an immediate relevance for prehistoric archaeology, for one of the main aims of prehistorians has been to establish an objective chronology for past events, using such basic methods as the analysis of stratigraphy and the application of absolute dating methods. Such processes have been fundamental to the creation of order among the material residues of the past. Moreover, those chronologies provide a framework within which quite different interpretations of the past can be considered. These may include the subjective understanding of time experienced by communities in prehistory, but that second approach may only rarely come within the competence of archaeologists.

It is easy to define the archaeological equivalent of the B-series. Unless archaeology can distinguish what came 'before' and 'after' particular events, it has no basis for proceeding, and it is that ability to define *sequence* on which much of the discussion in this book depends. Occasionally, it may be possible to consider the A-series too, but that will only be feasible in the light of an exact chronology. There are certain obvious clues; for example, buildings whose structure is based on the predictable movements of the heavenly bodies, or monuments that seem to have been built and dismantled according to a regular cycle (both are considered in Chapter 4). Otherwise what is most apparent is the way in which individual sites seem to have developed over extremely long periods or the distinctive manner in which individual styles of artefacts maintained their integrity over a similar time (these are also discussed in Chapters 3 and 4). If it is difficult to think about how ancient peoples envisaged the future development of their creations, they most certainly seem to have been aware of their own pasts. That is because its traces were ineradicable. Just as modern archaeologists are challenged by the survival of so many artefacts and monuments, people in antiquity could hardly have been unaware that they were living among the material remains of past generations, and those clues to their inheritance would have posed a challenge of its own. That might have been particularly true in those cases in which the forms of artefacts or structures resembled those that were still being made. In Gell's terms, those artefacts can be arranged in sequence in conformity with the B-series, but they may also have played a part in the subjective appreciation of time represented by the A-series.

At that point the distinction between history and prehistory becomes particularly important. Historians can investigate the past using the recorded testimony of witnesses from the period in question. That evidence may be partial or biased, but they can often tell this by comparing different versions of the same events. That is one of the methods permitted by the development of writing and, most especially, by the dissemination of printed texts (Goody 1977; Ong 1988;

Hutton 1993). Prehistorians are denied the same advantage and are forced to study the evidence of material things. It is only by considering how these might have been associated together in the past that it is possible to suggest how they were related to human lives. In this case the main sources of bias are those introduced by the researchers themselves.

People in prehistory will have had various perceptions of their own pasts and futures. It is unlikely that these will ever be known in any detail, but communities may have responded to the material remains of those pasts in rather similar ways to the archaeologist. Here the A- and B-series come together. How could societies have remembered their origins and earlier histories in the absence of documentation? One answer is that prehistoric groups maintained close links with the places where past events had happened and with forms of architecture and material culture which had been inherited from antiquity. Another possibility is through the promotion of oral traditions, but even this raises problems. If prehistoric societies are characterised by an absence of written texts, how stable were the traditions that must have taken their place?

This is a difficult question to discuss but it has been investigated by historians in recent years. It has also been of interest to literary scholars concerned with the stability of orally transmitted texts such as the poetry of Homer. The historians have considered the loss of information over time. Their conclusions vary but it seems clear from their work that oral traditions can become unstable or even corrupt within two hundred years (Henige 1974; Vansina 1985). Sometimes this happens still more rapidly. The loss of memory can be arrested by specialised techniques, for example the use of alliterative verse to record genealogies in Anglo-Saxon England, but for the most part there is an obvious loss of accuracy among recorded memories that extend far into the past (Sisam 1990). The same observation has been made in studies of oral literature. Although the performers may honestly believe that they are repeating the same material, ethnographic studies show that its content is steadily changing. This even happens when it is important to maintain the integrity of the 'text'. Beyond a certain point the past is incompletely known, and at this stage it may take on a rather different character. In a recent paper Gosden and Lock (1998) have compared the genealogical history that can still be recalled with interpretations of a still more distant past. They call this 'mythical history', for it was a history that could no longer be remembered accurately. Yet in many cases it was needed to interpret the material culture of the past.

Culture and material culture

The term material culture is both useful and puzzling at the same time. Culture is one of those words that have so many overlapping definitions that it almost defies discussion, but it took on one quite specific connotation in archaeology through the work of Childe (1956). For him, a culture was a unit of classification which could be treated as the equivalent of a prehistoric people. The way of arriving at such a classification was through the analysis of 'material culture', which he took to mean the buildings, monuments and portable artefacts that survived to be studied by prehistorians.

That link could be formed because of the workings of tradition. People made and used particular things in particular ways because they had been taught to do so. The same applied to the ways in which individual artefact types were designed and made. Behind each of these there were specific ideas, and so it was by following the connections between different styles of material culture over time and space that Childe was able to map the spread of ideas in ancient society. Because those ideas had to be taught and learned, it followed that archaeology could be used to trace the extent of traditional ways of doing and making things. Where many of these strands came together it was legitimate to postulate the existence of a society which shared a similar way of life. For Childe, that was a culture, like the Bell Beaker Culture or the Tumulus Culture.

Although this procedure might allow the archaeologist to people the past with extinct cultures, it is important to appreciate that Childe did not consider these variations to be explicit statements of local identities. Material culture was used in a more passive manner, and these learning networks existed on an almost unconscious level. They were the outward manifestation of shared ideas that may not have been articulated explicitly; still less were they used strategically. Because of this appeal to the existence of communities of shared ideas, processual archaeologists led by Binford (1965) dismissed the entire approach as 'palaeo-psychology'.

Such a negative reaction has not been supported by research in ethno-archaeology, for work in this field provides an opportunity to examine the distributions of artefact styles in relation to living populations. It investigates the ways in which traditions of making and using things are perceived by those communities. Such work supports Childe's original initiative but suggests a new interpretation of his findings. For example, Hodder's field investigation in Kenya has not led to the creation of a series of distinct cultures, marked by identifiable differences in material items (Hodder 1982). Rather, it suggests a more nuanced pattern in which artefact styles, styles of dress and different kinds of buildings can all be employed as means of communication. They are not the passive outcome of different learning networks, although those networks still remain an important factor. Instead, these separate media are employed as ways of affirming and interpreting some of the basic relationships in society, and they are used actively and openly. Thus they may be deployed to negotiate the relationships between kin and strangers, men and women, old and young, as well as those between different ethnic groups. Indeed, the whole study of ethnicity in archaeology has followed a rather similar course, with the result that this is another concept that may have been employed strategically (Jones 1997). An explicit statement of belonging to a particular human group may have had far more relevance than the question of biological descent.

If material culture is employed as a means of communication, it can only be understood in terms of the contexts in which it is used. Where Childe saw similarities and differences in prehistoric material culture as the outward manifestation of learning networks, we can now see them as playing a vital part in ancient social life. And, just as Childe interpreted these manifestations as an almost unconscious index of past identities, they may actually have been part of the very processes by which those identities were established and maintained.

But Childe did not regard the identification of cultures as his ultimate aim. Instead he used those cultures as building blocks in tracing the spread of peoples and ideas across prehistoric Europe. Chronology was just as important as geography. His programme is still being followed today, although it has been placed on a surer footing with the development of dating methods that only became widely available after his death. Curiously enough, the apparent continuities in material culture on which this work depends have not received as much critical examination as the distribution and associations of different artefact styles. Why were traditional practices in the production of material culture apparently so tenacious?

If material culture was used in an active manner, to distinguish between different groups or to highlight the significance of particular transactions, it does not seem likely that changes in its character over time would have been a passive affair. That would be to suggest that its distribution was meaningful while its chronological development was fortuitous. In fact less attention has been paid to the reasons for such changes. For the most part these have seemed obvious. Changes in the forms of artefacts and the built environment came about because of a growing mastery over the natural world. That is the premise behind the Three Age Model, and, on a smaller scale, it still retains its influence today. It is at the root of Binford's famous description of culture as an 'extra somatic means of adaptation' (Binford 1965). At the same time, people were open to experiment, assimilating ideas which they may have owed to other populations. That is one of the principles of diffusion, on which so much of Childe's chronology depends. Again, what seem to be significant changes may have happened simply because ideas were imperfectly transmitted over the generations, so that particular concepts and techniques were misunderstood and modified. In this case, the best comparison is with oral literature (Ong 1988). Such a matter of fact approach is entirely inadequate.

One pattern is very widespread and has provided the empirical basis for the method known as seriation. This is a technique of chronological analysis which depends on the observation, often made on deeply stratified sites, that different kinds of artefacts change their frequencies in an orderly manner. At first, they are rare, then their representation increases and, finally, it falls away as other types of object move through the same kind of sequence. Seriation depends on our ability to match those frequency curves in the most logical manner (Brainerd 1951). There is no question that this pattern is often found, but it has rarely been explained. Perhaps the most convincing model emphasises the social significance of these artefacts. Types that started out as novelties became more widely available until they had lost their original meanings. At that point their frequency decreased and they were replaced by new forms of material culture (Miller 1985: 184–96; Bradley 1988).

If this interpretation is correct, it suggests that material culture maintained a special significance *over time*. There is some evidence to support this view. It is worth considering the rates of change seen in prehistoric material culture. In some societies it seems as though changes in artefact styles were really quite rapid, while in others they are hard to detect, even over considerable periods. For instance, the ceramics of the Funnel Beaker Culture or the Linearbandkeramik have been seriated to provide a fine chronology in which significant changes became apparent over fairly short intervals (Midgley 1992; Lüning and Stehli 1994). By contrast, it is hard to find much stylistic variation among the pottery of earlier Neolithic Britain (Herne 1986). For 500 years there is little evidence of stylistic development beyond the adoption of a few decorative devices. In this case it seems as if there was an explicit intention to retain the forms associated with tradition.

The same problems apply to the forms of monuments. There are regions in which there is a wide range of variation and where it may be possible to discern a complex and steadily evolving sequence of types. The megaliths of Brittany would be a good example (Boujot and Cassen 1993). In other cases, the outward forms of monuments remained the same over enormous periods of time, no matter how much their functions may have varied. A good example is the use of causewayed enclosures in Neolithic Europe which may have extended across nearly 1500 years (Bradley 1998: chapter 5). The same is true of domestic architecture. Thus an Atlantic tradition of circular buildings maintained its integrity from at least the Copper Age to the Late Iron Age (Cunliffe 2001) while the Continental preference for rectangular houses extended continuously from the Neolithic period. There are few signs that these traditions took much account of one another, even though there are occasional settlements in which both forms are found together.

The most likely explanation is that such continuities were used just as strategically as the variations in material culture mapped by Childe. People did not make artefacts or build structures according to a traditional format because they were unable to think of anything else. Rather, they did so as one way of adhering to tradition and maintaining links with what they knew of their past. Making a decorated pot according to a time-honoured formula was an act of remembering just as much as visiting and maintaining a burial mound. In the same way, choosing to break with traditional practice may also have involved an explicit position on the relationship between the present and the past:

> Where chronological sequences of styles can reliably be built by strati-
> graphic or chronometric means, an attempt can be made to infer the
> narratives according to which past agents constructed their lives. I am not
> referring here to individual plots or brief histories. Rather, I refer to . . . the

large-scale narratives . . . in which we are all enmeshed. . . . It is particularly
in the expressive, rather than the technological, areas of cultures that
narratives are told.

(Hodder 1993: 269)

Because material culture is used expressively, it is created from an awareness
of what already exists, or has existed in the recent past. Changes in its character
may not have arisen by chance and could actually have resulted from a deliberate
attempt to emphasise similarities or contrasts with tradition. That is the 'rhetoric'
of material culture and it is in this sense that such sequences embody narratives
or plots. One example has been suggested by Hodder (1993) in a study of the
pottery from Sitagroi in northern Greece. Here, he argues, the changing forms
of the pottery on the site could have been used to comment on that made in
earlier phases.

About remembering

Such arguments may be difficult to substantiate, but it is true that the whole of
human culture depends on the workings of memory. That is because of the way
in which traditions are learnt and assimilated. They may not have been taught in
the way that characterises modern education. Rather, the very process of living
in a traditional society would have inculcated a sense of the appropriate forms of
behaviour. That might have been acquired in at least two different ways. First, it
might have come about through what has been called bodily practice: participa-
tion in rituals and ceremonies which could be assimilated through performance
until those routines became second nature. In that case people acted instinctively
rather than intellectually (Connerton 1989). The same applies to the role of
material culture, which might provide a sequence of cues to the appropriate
forms of behaviour in society: the correct places to locate oneself within a building, the right material items to employ in particular contexts, the appropriate
clothes to wear on different occasions (Bourdieu 1977). These conventions
would be learnt by experience and by watching other people, and might never
have been codified at all. They developed an awareness of the right kinds of
conduct, and much of this information was provided by the ways in which
material things were organised, from the layout of a building to the ceramic
vessels used for serving a meal.

A second way in which social memory is developed is through the building of
monuments intended to perpetuate a particular view of the world. In modern
society this is akin to the preparation of documents, and for that reason the
process has been described as 'inscription' (Connerton 1989). The work of
historians contributes to this process, and so, to a lesser extent, do the writings of
archaeologists. This kind of social memory is enshrined in public buildings,
statues and works of art. These may have acquired a stability from the media
in which they were composed. While they might have been made with the

same intentions as oral narratives, they need not have changed their form over the generations. That is not to say that their meanings would have remained equally stable.

Each of these approaches created a different kind of memory. What has been called inscription led to the creation of a durable material culture, and this was often available to be interpreted for some time afterwards. That applies mainly to the establishment of settlements, monuments and other substantial structures whose very organisation may have encoded wider ideas about the world, but, in principle, it can also apply to the making of smaller objects, some of which could have circulated for lengthy periods after they were made.

The creation of memory though human behaviour is described by the rather cumbersome term 'incorporated practices' (Connerton 1989). It takes a quite different form, as such activity may leave no tangible remains behind. One way in which this happens is through the destruction of material items. Certain objects are removed from circulation so that they no longer pose a problem of interpretation. Instead, a memory of that event remains and can be transmitted orally. Sometimes such events are repeated, so that each episode of cultural destruction is renewed after an interval, in that way enhancing the recollection of the original transaction. That process takes the paradoxical form of 'remembering by forgetting' (Küchler 1987 and 1999).

Both contributed to the archaeological record. The process of inscription poses fewer problems because it depends on the survival of a durable material culture. Indeed, the sheer persistence of monuments or other modifications of the landscape was one of the elements out of which prehistoric archaeology was formed. On the other hand, the creation of memory by destroying things may also have consequences for prehistorians. Many of those objects were removed from circulation through their deposition in the ground. This may have removed them from the everyday experience of people in the past but it has ensured their survival to the present day, so that now they dominate the professional literature. Much of the intact metalwork on which Childe's chronology depended was only available to be studied because it had been taken out of circulation deliberately. In one sense this biases the material record, but, in another, it enriches the work of archaeologists in a way that no one would have predicted in the early years of the discipline.

Each process would have demanded interpretation even in the prehistoric period. There is no doubt that people would have been aware of the built fabric of their own past in the landscapes in which they lived. Even if they had chosen to ignore it, it would still have posed a problem. At the same time, they would have encountered some of the concealed deposits of artefacts mentioned earlier, although they may never have intended to do so. They would have found these in the process of clearing land, while opening new graves in older burial mounds or in rebuilding their settlements, and again they would have faced a similar challenge. Like archaeologists from at least the time of Darwin, they would have been forced to use these scraps of ancient material culture to understand their place in the world. It is that distinctive process that I shall explore in this book.

The past and the future in the past

Historians seem to agree that oral traditions lose their stability within 200 years unless specialised techniques are developed for the accurate transmission of memory between the generations. That same estimate comes close to the limits of resolution of most prehistoric chronologies.

For that reason it has been difficult to follow the growth and dissolution of traditions with the accuracy that we would wish, although improvements in dating methods may one day bring that objective within our grasp. In the same way, it may not be possible for archaeologists to recover past conceptions of time save in the most exceptional circumstances. Both recent studies that do address this issue – Gosden's *Social Being and Time*, and Thomas's *Time, Culture and Identity* – are forced to operate in rather abstract terms (Gosden 1994; Thomas 1996). As a result, Gosden can make little use of the intricacies of the archaeological record and his reworking of a number of existing case studies involves a certain loss of detail. Thomas's study moves in the other direction. He does offer a fine-grained analysis of several bodies of archaeological data, but it is quite difficult to link this with the discussion of twentieth century philosophy that forms the first part of his book. Both authors overlook a more immediate issue: the many different *practices* by means of which ancient peoples reacted to the surviving remains of antiquity. Such remains would have been particularly significant as oral traditions lapsed, and, unlike the more abstract topics tackled by both these writers, such practices left obvious traces for archaeologists to study. These empirical patterns have been largely ignored, and it is time to investigate them now.

The studies in this book bring many of these theoretical issues to bear on the results of fieldwork. They consider a series of relationships between societies and their understanding of the past. Most of them are based on concrete examples taken from different areas of prehistoric Europe (Figures 1.2 and 1.3). Chapter 2 begins the sequence by investigating events far removed from the people who celebrated them. These are origin myths, and they are illustrated by two examples from Neolithic Europe, one concerned with the symbolic role of long houses and the earthwork monuments that took their place, and the other with the menhirs that are such a feature of the Atlantic coastline. These statues had a changing history, starting in the open air and later being incorporated inside megalithic tombs. The two case studies, one from Central and Northern Europe, and the other from Southern and Western Europe, also allow us to compare the basic processes by which social memory is created. In one case this happened through the use of monumental structures, and in the other there is evidence for the destruction and concealment of images.

Chapter 3 considers the immediate past of prehistoric people. First, it discusses their use of material culture and emphasises the importance of working out the

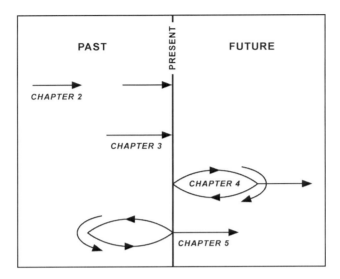

Figure 1.2 An outline of the structure of this book.

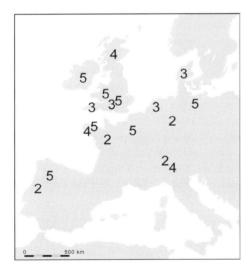

Figure 1.3 The regions of Europe considered in this book.

Note
The numbers relate to the separate chapters.

biographies of different kinds of artefacts. The treatment of particular objects during the course of their life histories is particularly important here, and the first section discusses the uses of pottery and metalwork in Scandinavia and the British Isles. In each case these cannot be understood without some knowledge of how these artefacts were related to practices in the past. The discussion extends to the treatment of houses and occupation sites in the routines of everyday life and focuses on the ways in which buildings were replaced by others during the history of individual settlements. It also considers their relationship to burials and field systems. These examples are drawn from the prehistory of Northern Europe. The discussion then turns to the ways of reworking entire landscapes. It investigates the distinctive archaeology of Dartmoor in South-West England and the transformation of this region during the Bronze Age.

After this, Chapter 4 is concerned with monumental architecture and with projects that may have been meant to influence the memories of later generations. The examples are taken from a number of regions of Scotland, Italy and Northern France and trace the distinctive features of different kinds of projects. First, there were monuments that were destroyed and rebuilt, perhaps on a regular cycle. These are illustrated by a series of recently excavated monuments in Britain. The second case is rather similar. This is where monuments were intended to have a limited life before they were closed or abandoned. By contrast, other examples continued to be built and reinterpreted over enormous spans of time. These are illustrated by the archaeology of two famous monument complexes in Continental Europe: Aosta in Northern Italy, and Carnac in North-West France. In each case monument building took on a life of its own, and both these projects went far beyond the intentions of those who inaugurated them.

That leads logically to Chapter 5, which is concerned with the ancient rediscovery of the past. It begins with past reactions to older artefacts in the Roman and Medieval periods. These are illustrated by examples from Spain, Northern France and Wales. It then develops into an account of the different ways in which long abandoned monuments might be reclaimed during later periods. This involves three short case studies: the reuse of prehistoric burial monuments in Northern Germany; the contrasting contexts in which La Tène funerary enclosures were adopted on the Continent and in Lowland England; and, finally, the development of the Irish royal site at Tara between the Neolithic period and the Early Middle Ages. Such processes extend into the historical period and even lead directly to the practice of archaeology itself.

Having begun this book with an episode from the early life of Charles Darwin, in the final chapter I turn to the career of a near-contemporary of his, Sir Richard Colt Hoare. He began as a student of Roman culture, but later became one of the first people in Europe to undertake systematic excavation and survey at prehistoric sites. I shall consider the influence of both men on the ways in which field archaeology has developed, and the new conceptions of time that grew out of that work.

Chapter 2

Acknowledging antiquity
Towards an archaeology of distant origins

The enigma of arrival

One of the features that unites particular communities is their sense of sharing a common origin. That is the literal meaning of the adjective *aboriginal*, which, in the dictionary definition, suggests that specific people have 'exist[ed] in a land from the earliest times' (*Oxford Concise English Dictionary*). They could even have been created there, and their ancestors might still be present in some form. But in other cases their origins are considered to be as distant in space as they are in time. People may trace their roots back to settlement from quite another area, which is why the narrative often turns on the travels of heroic forebears.

Such beliefs are so widespread that it is surprising how much they overlap. That is surely because they perform a role in sustaining the self-image of an educated elite; those accounts are not subject to the rules of evidence applied by modern historians. A good example is one of the foundation myths of the Classical world, set down by Virgil in his epic poem, the *Aeneid*. This follows the travels of its hero from the sack of Troy to Italy, where his descendants were to build the city of Rome. Virgil had the example of Homer to emulate, and the Greek poet's own epics, the *Iliad* and the *Odyssey*, drew on some of the same events. The *Iliad* followed the course of the Trojan War and, like the *Aeneid*, the *Odyssey* described the travels of one of the protagonists after that conflict was over. Homer's work was first written down at a time of political change in Greece and may have offered an historical justification for some of those developments (Morris 1986).

A number of the same characters appear again in the origin myths of Northern Europe. The genealogies of the royal houses draw on an improbable selection of sources, including the Classical pantheon, Nordic gods and figures from the Old Testament, yet again they feature one of the participants in the Trojan War (Sisam 1990). Less well known is another story recorded about 1136 by Geoffrey of Monmouth in his *History of the Kings of Britain*. This tells of Brutus, the grandson of Aeneas who was destined to cause the deaths of both his parents before he was exiled from Italy. His travels led him through Africa and Aquitania until eventually he arrived in Britain, landing at Totnes during what would now be called the Iron Age. Here his descendants ruled until the invasion of Julius Caesar reunited the British with the Roman people. According to Nennius, the sons and cousins of Brutus included Francus, Romanus, Albanus, Gothus, Burgundus, Langobardus and Vandalus. These relationships would have established links between Aeneas, the Trojan War and the genesis of other political groups in the Early Middle Ages (Creighton 2000: 138–45). There were similar narratives involving figures from Roman history in Ireland and Early Medieval Wales and at one time the kings of Scotland traced their lineage back to the Pharaohs of Egypt. This was a modest claim compared with that put forward by Sir Thomas Urquhart of Cromarty, the first translator of Rabelais into English. His book, *A Peculiar Promptuary of Time*, published in 1652, traces his own genealogy across 143 generations back to Adam and Eve (Boston 1975).

In some cases the stories recount the exploits of particular individuals who are celebrated as the founders of different communities. In others their origins may be concerned as much with distant places. A good example is provided by the Irish *Book of Invasions*, which describes the successive waves of immigrants who colonised the country (Champion 1982). Another case may be the belief, documented by the historian Bede, that the Early Medieval Picts who lived in what is now Scotland were directly descended from the Scythians of the Russian steppes (Wainwright 1953: 10–11). Such myths are very common, but not all these stories need feature human beings. Some of the Anglo-Saxon kings claimed descent from pagan gods and such accounts often feature other kinds of creatures: mythical animals and spirits which can be threatening or benign. Even in these cases the basic principle is much the same. These narratives account for the origins of particular groups in society and provide a charter for their activities.

A well researched example is found in Hugh-Jones's book, *From the Milk River*, which is concerned with the ethnography of the north-west Amazon (Hugh-Jones 1979). It deals with the lives and beliefs of the Piri-paraná people of modern Columbia. They live in long houses close to the course of the river, and the river itself provides a vital metaphor as it traces the course originally taken by their ancestors when they moved upstream. Towards its source in the west is the forest, which is associated with evil spirits. To the east is the area from which the ancestors came. At the same time, the path of the river can be interpreted in other ways. It also represents a giant snake, an anaconda, different segments of which are associated with different parts of society. The east is connected with chiefs and the west with servants. Other roles include dancers, chanters, warriors and shamans. Their locations along the length of the 'river-snake' link the dancers to the ancestral world and the warriors to human society. The shamans are closer to the forest spirits in the headwaters of the Milk River.

The same symbolic scheme applies to the layout of the long house. Thus the east door of the building is related to the ancestors and the west door to the forest and the wild. The same division refers to the differences between women and men. The interior of the house is divided between a masculine space towards one entrance and a kitchen area at the opposite end which is a female preserve. At the same time, the entire structure is aligned on the axis of the river and is placed in between the water and the forest.

Hugh-Jones explains how these different levels are related to one another:

> The universe is treated as a conceptual construction which contains the activity and power associated with ancestral creation. In order to contact this alternative reality, people must transpose the system of the universe with its creative processes onto the concrete systems which they are able to control, or at least change, through practical action. To do this *they construct their houses to represent the universe.*
>
> (1979: 235 [my emphasis])

On every level their existence is also permeated by the events of a mythical past:

> The house only lives when people are inside it; the sites on the ancestral journey upstream did not exist until the ancestors stopped at them; the rivers did not flow until they had been trodden out by the ancestors.
>
> (ibid.: 237)

Thus the structure of the settlement and the wider landscape can only be comprehended in relation to an origin myth.

There are a number of reasons why that example is so intriguing. It is a classic case in which the organisation of material culture – in this case a domestic building – has to be understood in relation to ideas referring to the distant past. Such buildings were far more than residential structures, for, as Hugh-Jones says, they were models of the universe that also documented the history of the people who lived inside them. Those houses could certainly be interpreted in terms of spatial organisation and this might bring to light some of the concerns that they expressed – the important distinction between the river and the forest, for instance, or that between women and men – but these would be largely meaningless without some insight into the ways in which they were woven into the occupants' ideas about their origins. Without some understanding of the part played by their ancestors, any analysis would be foreshortened.

But can such complicated issues be investigated by prehistorians, whose only informants are dead? In this chapter I shall explore two case studies from Neolithic Europe which could shed light on the ways in which ancient people may also have thought about their origins. Such analyses will always be incomplete because the evidence is limited, but they do serve to show how social memories could have been created in very different ways.

Leaving home

My first study concerns the Linear Pottery Culture, one of the two key elements in the Neolithic of North-West Europe. (The other, Cardial Ware, is considered later in this chapter.)

The Linear Pottery Culture or *Linearbandkeramik* is often considered to epitomise the agricultural colonisation of Europe, but in some respects it is anomalous. It seems to have originated in Central Europe against a background that is best documented among the well preserved settlement sites of the Balkans (Bailey 2000: chapters 2–5). In Western Europe it retained its distinctive identity for a remarkable length of time, between about 5500 and 5000 BC, and extended over a very large area before it began to fragment into a series of smaller regional traditions. Once they had run their course, from approximately 4000 BC, there were equally drastic changes in the nature of subsistence and settlement, and after that time occupation sites are less well documented than specialised earthwork monuments (Whittle 1996: chapter 7).

Although the Linearbandkeramik has been interpreted in terms of agricultural colonisation, it is actually rather unusual. It is certainly true that its settlements are characterised by enormous buildings – long houses – and that these are largely confined to the most fertile loess soils, yet this approach is somehow deceptive. The houses themselves are almost too big, too monumental, with the result that they are difficult to interpret entirely in terms of the routines of daily life (Bradley 2001). Moreover, the highly specialised pattern of settlement described in so much of the literature may also be misleading, for ecological considerations suggest that some of the livestock would have needed additional areas of grazing land beyond the limits of the loess where the evidence of occupation sites is much less substantial (Bakels 1978; Gregg 1988).

Moreover, such a functional approach to Linearbandkeramik settlement is difficult to reconcile with either the system from which it had emerged or the social practices that succeeded it. The major settlements of the Balkans were permeated by ritual activity and cannot be understood in such simple terms. They contain a range of artefacts including clay figures and decorated pottery which seem to have been deliberately broken before they were deposited in a highly structured manner (Chapman, J. 2000). Furthermore, the house sites are accompanied by human remains. Some are intact burials, but there are also isolated bones that may have circulated in a similar manner to the figurines. The buildings seem to have been burned down every generation with their contents inside them, perhaps when one of the occupants died (Stepanovic 1997). Afterwards the houses were replaced in practically the same positions: a process that created the mounds of settlement debris known as *tells*.

Towards the opposite end of the sequence it is equally difficult to adopt a determinist model. Agricultural expansion seems to have faltered; some of the last Linear Pottery settlements and their successors are associated with earthwork enclosures; and, in contrast to the characteristic pattern on the loess, the remains of residential buildings become increasingly difficult to find. There may have been a greater emphasis on mobility, even a widening of the resource base, but it is hardly enough to explain all these changes. Most striking of all, a range of mortuary monuments developed whose characteristic forms echoed those of the massive long houses that were no longer being built (Bradley 1998: chapters

3–4). The same applies to the evidence from the earthwork enclosures (ibid.: chapter 5). Whereas the first of these were associated with settlements and could even surround groups of long houses, the later examples were more closely connected with the dead and the supernatural. In this chapter I suggest that they were used as ceremonial centres.

Given the distinctive character of this sequence, it does not seem likely that the organisation of the Linear Pottery settlements was governed entirely by functional considerations. It may have had a subtler significance, and that may even provide a reason why it was so uniform over such a considerable area. Even more important is a question that arises out of the argument in Chapter 1. Why were the components of the Linearbandkeramik settlements so significant that they remained almost unchanged for well over 500 years? That cannot have happened by chance. Surely, their significance extended beyond everyday considerations.

The key to this discussion is provided by the long houses, which hardly altered their form during the course of the Linear Pottery Culture, although, like the ceramics, they underwent important developments in later phases. Generally speaking, these houses survive as settings of post holes. No floor surfaces are preserved and the only features to contain large numbers of artefacts are the borrow pits which flank the sides of the buildings. These probably provided the clay needed to plaster the walls. In Western Europe (the area considered in this account) the classic Linearbandkeramik long house has three structural elements, with a door at one end (Figure 2.1). That tripartite division is not so apparent in regions further to the east (Mattheuser 1991; Coudart 1998).

Long houses of various forms play a persistent role in European prehistory and continued in use into the Middle Ages. It has been particularly tempting to draw on that comparison in order to interpret the separate parts of these buildings (Modderman 1988: 96). In Linear Pottery houses the most massive construction was the first segment, which is represented by an array of large post holes. It has often been suggested that this section of the long house may have been built on two floors and could have included a granary.

The middle section of the Neolithic long house provides a more open space, which is normally regarded as the principal living area. Beyond it again is the final compartment, which was generally built in a different technique from the other parts of the structure. Instead of spaced posts, the outer wall was made up of a continuous series of planks set in a foundation trench. Because this was so firmly bedded, the end section of the long house has been interpreted as a byre.

This simple functional scheme is quite inadequate. It receives little support from phosphate analysis or from the analysis of artefact distributions on excavated sites (Stäuble and Lüning 1999). Moreover, it raises some major practical problems, for while it would have been eminently reasonable to store cereals close to the entrance of the building, it seems most unlikely that livestock had to cross the entire living area before they could reach the byre. In any case the analogy with later structures is misleading. They are divided into segments with

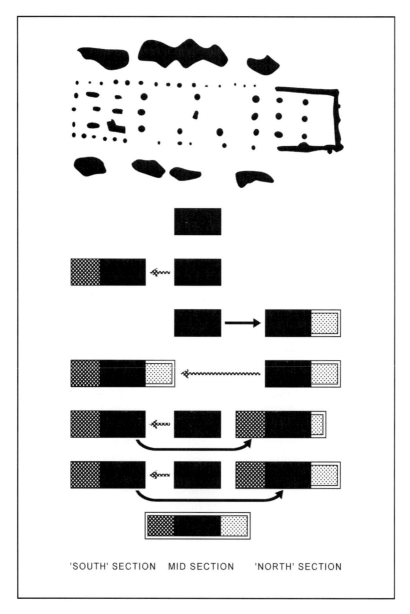

'SOUTH' SECTION   MID SECTION   'NORTH' SECTION

Figure 2.1 Outline plan of a Linearbandkeramik long house at Geleen, Netherlands.
Source: information from Waterbolk (1959).

Notes
The block diagrams emphasise the tripartite organisation of space inside these buildings. The
diagrams summarise the logical relationships between the central section and those towards
the north and south. Bold arrows indicate sequences that can be documented archaeologically.
The faint arrows indicate other sequences of development which are possible but conjectural.

distinct living areas and cattle stalls, but these were entered through separate doors in the sides of the building (Fokkens and Roymans 1991).

In fact the Linearbandkeramik long houses are far from uniform and by no means all these structures contain the same number of elements. That has to be explained. Subject to what is said later, these buildings are aligned roughly north–south and in the discussion that follows I shall use a neutral terminology in which the 'granary', the 'living area' and the 'byre' are referred to as the 'southern', 'central' and 'northern' sections, respectively. All the buildings seem to possess a central section, but the other two elements do not always occur, and even when they do so they may not be found together (Coudart 1998). Still more important, there is no evidence that most of the major long houses had been constructed in a single operation (the obvious exceptions are some rather unusual buildings bounded by a plank-built wall around their entire perimeter). The northern section is sometimes misaligned, suggesting that it could have been added at a later date (ibid.: 74).

This raises the possibility that individual houses were constructed incrementally. Since the central section is ubiquitous and is the only component found on its own, it seems likely that it provided the original core. As we have seen, the northern section might sometimes be a later addition, and in virtually every case its erection brought expansion in this direction to an end; there is very little evidence that this part of the house was ever extended or rebuilt. It is harder to discuss the relationship between the central area and the massive southern section which seems to mark the position of the door. It may also have been a later development, but there is no way of proving it.

One reason for taking this view is that on some sites the internal sub-divisions of the long house were clearly emphasised by the organisation of the external borrow pits. Had the long houses been unitary constructions, it would seem logical for these pits to continue along the full extent of the side walls, but this is not particularly common. Instead, they can be broken into segments and the causeways of unexcavated soil generally correspond to the positions of the section divisions within the structure of the house. The point is important as the division between the southern and central sections would not have been apparent from the appearance of the outer wall. The plank-built northern section, on the other hand, would have been recognisable from outside. Again it is possible to think of practical explanations – Simonin (1997), for instance, suggests that the gaps between the borrow pits correspond to the positions of windows in the house – but the symbolic importance of these divisions may have been important, too. In the Paris Basin children had been buried in these pits (Veit 1996).

It seems as if some of the houses increased in size over time and that this process was communicated to an outside observer by the organisation of the borrow pits. The process of expansion was by no means uniform from one site to another and the excavated evidence is such that certain practices probably can be identified, while others must remain conjectural. Whatever the relationship between the southern and central sections of the long house, it is clear that the construction of the northern segment precluded any further extension at that end of the building. It may be one reason why this part of the structure was bounded by a continuous wall of planks set in a bedding trench, for it would have been more difficult to replace a wall of this kind than the other divisions within the building. In a sense, the creation of that 'closed' northern section walled with planks signified that the development of the building was complete. At the same time, we have already seen that the central section of the long house is the only part that can be found in isolation. Clearly this was the basic element from which a more elaborate structure might develop. A point of considerable importance is the observation that the shorter houses found in Linearbandkeramik settlements were most common when the occupation of particular sites was coming to an end (Coudart 1998: 48–9). In that respect, they were 'incomplete'. When the settlement was relocated, the growth of individual buildings may have ceased before it could run its course.

Again it is tempting to look for practical explanations. It is certainly true that it is easy to extend square or rectangular houses (Hunter-Anderson 1977), but the question is why it should have been necessary to do so, rather than build another one. The answer is surely connected with social organisation. There are numerous precedents in the ethnographic record for large groups of people choosing to live together under one roof (Carsten and Hugh-Jones 1995; Birdwell-Pheasant and Lawrence-Zuñiga 1999). The essential feature that underlies many of these examples is the principle that the house should grow organically. The number of occupants increases as the building provides a home for different generations, so that the house itself becomes a historical document, tracing the life course of the people who live within it. This is a model that has been applied to the Iron Age long houses of the Netherlands (Gerritsen 1999), and in the case of Linearbandkeramik buildings it might help to explain why the positions of the internal sub-divisions were so important that they were highlighted by external borrow pits. By this means a stranger could be informed of the history of its inhabitants.

A purely practical approach would need to consider other questions. How long did it take for such a house to assume its final form? A substantial building of this kind would not last for ever: how was it repaired? What would happen as the oldest inhabitants died and the number of occupants diminished? Were segments of these buildings abandoned piecemeal? Did they change their roles, or would the time come when it was better to begin the cycle again, by replacing the original building and salvaging what material could be used?

It is by putting the questions in these terms that we come to realise how far the long houses of the Linear Pottery Culture departed from such a pragmatic approach to domestic life. Several observations are vitally important here. Somewhat unexpectedly, there is very little evidence that these massive structures were repaired on a significant scale, nor do the records of well excavated sites suggest that large timbers were salvaged from the long houses when they were finally abandoned. In fact, the abandonment of individual buildings seems to have taken place while they were structurally sound, suggesting that this decision was influenced by less material factors (Bradley 1998: chapter 3). Perhaps the houses could no longer be occupied after particular occupants had died, as may have happened in the Neolithic settlements of the Balkans where individual buildings seem to have been burnt down every generation (Stepanovic 1997). The life span of the long houses seems to have been rather similar, but there the comparison ends. In South-East Europe each building was replaced on practically the same site, contributing to the formation of a settlement mound or tell. In North-West Europe, however, it seems to have been important to replace each of the long houses in a completely different position. In fact the dwellings of the living and the abandoned houses associated with the dead often follow the same alignment and are spaced at approximately equal intervals across the settled area (Figure 2.2). It seems likely that the positions of abandoned buildings were remembered and respected even after their structures had decayed (Bradley 1998: chapter 3).

That suggests another way in which the form of the Linearbandkeramik settlement might have documented the history of its inhabitants. The appearance of individual long houses might have traced their fortunes across the generations, while the entire settlement with its distinctive configuration of 'living' and 'dead' houses could have made a similar statement about the community as a whole.

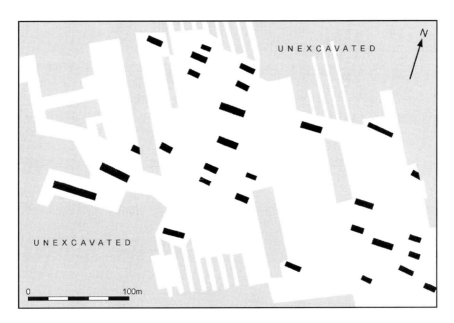

Figure 2.2 The spacing of long houses in the Linearbandkeramik settlement at Cuiry-les-Chaudardes, Northern France, emphasising the common alignment of the buildings.

Source: information from Coudart (1998).

There may be yet another level on which the distinctive form of these settlements maintained social memory. For convenience I have described the components of the Neolithic long house in relation to its prevailing axis. In general terms they contained a 'northern' and 'southern' section, as well as a central living area, although in fact their orientations are more varied. Again this has been explained in purely practical terms. Marshall (1981) has argued that their construction was aerodynamic and they were aligned in relation to the directions of the prevailing winds (Figure 2.3).

At first sight this seems a reasonable idea, but the analysis on which it was based depends on a small and unrepresentative sample of Linearbandkeramik occupation sites. A more extensive analysis by Coudart provides no support for this suggestion, for on a larger geographical scale there is little relationship between the long axis of these houses and local wind directions (1998: 88–90).

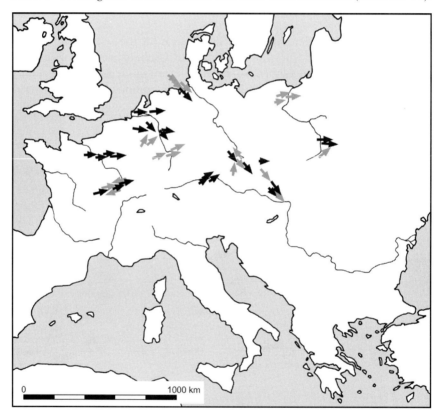

Figure 2.3 Prevailing wind directions in the regions with Linearbandkeramik long houses.

Source: information from Coudart (1998).

Note

The bold arrows indicate the main wind directions in summer and the faint arrows those in winter.

Perhaps that is not surprising as long houses constructed within small clearings would not have been as vulnerable to wind pressure as their later counterparts in a more open landscape.

At the same time, there does seem to be a certain regularity in the orientation of the Neolithic buildings. In Central Europe they do follow an approximate north–south axis, but beyond that area they are often deflected towards the north-west and west (Figure 2.4). Coudart emphasises the plank-built sections of these structures and suggests that they were facing the nearest coastline. As a matter of geography that is certainly correct, but the distances involved are up to 600 kilometres and, while there is evidence for contacts between the Linear Pottery Culture and coastal hunter-gatherers, it is not uniformly distributed around the margins of North-West Europe, so it is difficult to see how such

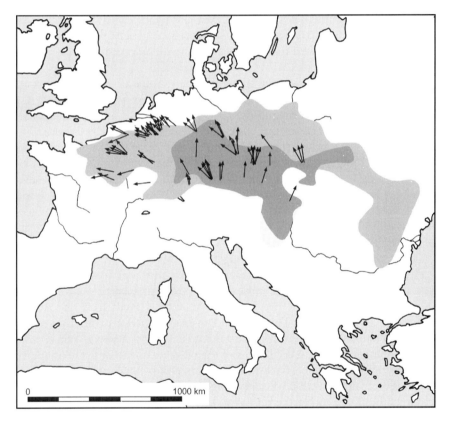

Figure 2.4 The chronological extension of the Linearbandkeramik according to Lüning, Kloos and Albert (1989).

Notes
The denser shading indicates the earlier phases of settlement and the lighter shading its subsequent expansion. The arrows show the orientations of Neolithic long houses, as documented by Kind (1989) and Coudart (1998).

detailed knowledge might have been acquired. Coudart also suggests that the orientation of these buildings was influenced by cosmological factors. This is entirely plausible, but perhaps it was the orientation of the doorways rather than the far ends of these houses that was most significant.

It is not clear how the Linear Pottery Culture became established over such a large area of Europe, and the respective contributions made by agricultural colonists and indigenous hunter-gatherers remain a subject for debate. On the other hand, the chronology and extent of the Linearbandkeramik are not in dispute. Lüning and his colleagues have identified a gradual process of settlement extending from Central Europe towards the north-west, with further areas towards the west and north-east (Lüning, Kloos and Albert 1989). This is supported by ceramic chronology and radiocarbon dating. It is relevant to the present discussion because the basic sequence is so closely allied to the orientation of the long houses. With very few exceptions, their doorways appear to be aligned on the areas that had previously been occupied (see Figure 2.4). Whether or not these buildings were the dwellings of an immigrant population, *they seem to acknowledge an area of origin that had been settled in the past.*

There are further reasons for taking this view. Some of the settlements are accompanied by nearby cemeteries. These can be poorly preserved but in a number of cases, particularly in the Paris Basin, there is a clear relationship between the orientation of the bodies and that of the nearby houses. The corpse may be buried on the same alignment as the house, so that the head corresponds to the position of the door. In other cases the body is laid out on a different axis from these buildings, but again the head is facing in the same direction as the building (Mattheuser 1991: 17–23). Both kinds of burial suggest that the long house was aligned on the areas settled during earlier phases (for a similar interpretation, based on strontium isotope analysis, see Price *et al.* 2001).

There may be another way of investigating this relationship. Is there any direct evidence that relations were maintained with Central and South-East Europe during this phase? One of the most distinctive characteristics of the Neolithic period is the long-distance movement of Spondylus shells from the Aegean (Müller 1997) (Figure 2.5). This took place over a long period of time, but among the later examples are finds from Linearbandkeramik cemeteries, where these shells are associated with the burials of the older members of the community. The overall distribution of these finds traces one of the routes along which farming was introduced into Europe and extends over an enormous distance from the Black Sea to Northern France. The shells do not seem to have played any practical role and their real importance may have depended on their distant origin and their association with regions that had been settled in the remote past. Perhaps they are tangible evidence for a connection between the settlements of the Linear Pottery Culture and those ancestral homelands on which the houses were aligned.

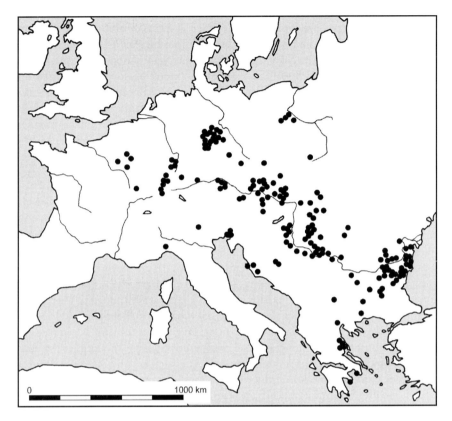

Figure 2.5 The distribution of Spondylus shells in Neolithic and Copper Age Europe.
Source: information from Müller (1997).

Memories in earth and stone

At the end of the Linearbandkeramik there are signs of fragmentation and a number of local pottery styles developed instead of the broadly uniform repertoire that had existed before. Long houses continued to be used. Again they could take slightly different forms, with a greater emphasis on a trapezoidal ground plan, but in some areas, especially in Northern France, borrow pits were still constructed along the flanks of these buildings. Some of the later settlements were associated with ditched enclosures, a new form of construction that had first appeared towards the end of the Linear Pottery Culture.

By about 4000 BC the practice of building long houses had been largely discontinued and with it the grouping of buildings into substantial settlements also came to an end. At first sight that marks a radical break in the adoption of agriculture in Europe, especially since it was at this time that Neolithic material culture was introduced into new regions. These were areas which had previously been occupied by hunter-gatherers, and while they had been content to receive exotic artefacts across the agricultural frontier, it seems doubtful whether many of these communities had undergone significant changes as a result of these contacts (Sherratt 1990). Now the situation was very different. Domesticated resources were increasingly adopted in regions extending northwards into Scandinavia and westwards to Britain and Ireland. The same process had already affected the coast of Northern France (Whittle 1996: chapters 6 and 7).

It is not clear that the residential pattern of earlier periods was maintained. As we have seen, long houses went out of use and it is often difficult to identify the domestic buildings that took their place. Even when they can be found, it does not seem likely that people were living in large villages, and yet the archaeology of this period preserves two very curious echoes of the earlier settlement system.

The first was originally identified in North-East Europe and it is the evidence from that region that dominated the discussion until recently (Hodder 1990: 145). This is the creation of elongated earthen mounds, whose form and orientation seem to follow those of the long houses that had been built within the recent past. Indeed, in Poland there are entire cemeteries of such mounds organised on similar lines to the settlements themselves. There is controversy over the precise relationship between these earthworks and their prototypes. They occur on different sites from one another and the first long barrows may be later in date than the long houses that they seem to copy (Midgley 1992: 463–4). Moreover, these monuments were geographically far removed from the long barrows of North-West Europe.

Recent work in Northern France has established a more compelling relationship between the last long houses and earthworks of this kind. At Balloy, Seine-et-Marne, there was a settlement associated with long houses, several of which were directly overlain by elongated mortuary enclosures or, more probably, mounds (Mordant 1998; Midgley 2000) (Figure 2.6). The latter were associated with a series of individual burials. There may have been a short interval between the abandonment of the houses and the construction of these earthworks but the fact that the newly built barrows shared the size, spacing and orientation of those buildings means that the people who constructed them understood the layout of the older settlement. That was why individual houses were replaced directly by these earthworks. In that sense the houses of the living were supplanted by the houses of the dead.

Whether or not the sequence in North-East Europe followed a similar course, this relationship has important consequences for an understanding of Neolithic archaeology, for it is precisely when the long house disappeared as a building form that earthworks of this kind were first created: the same basic idea was transferred from one medium to another. In place of a long rectangular dwelling, which was often flanked by borrow pits, a mound of similar proportions was constructed to cover the remains of the dead. That earthwork was sometimes enclosed by a ditch. It was as if the mortuary monuments copied the attributes of domestic buildings and rendered them in a more durable form (Bradley 1998: chapter 3).

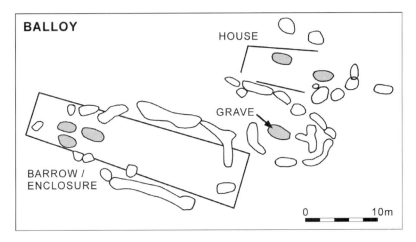

Figure 2.6 The remains of long mounds or long enclosures overlying the sites of houses at Balloy, Northern France.

Source: information from Mordant (1998).

It would be wrong to over emphasise the evidence of these particular sites, for the specific relationships suggested in Poland and Northern France have yet to be identified in other areas, although that is not to deny that some long mounds were built over the remains of settlements of other kinds. In fact it is the rarity of this convergence that is really intriguing. Long houses and long mounds have almost mutually exclusive distributions and their chronologies scarcely overlap. These monuments to the dead replaced the dwellings of the living and carried the structural principles of the Linearbandkeramik and its immediate successors into new regions of the continent. The specific transformation observed on a site like Balloy is important because it encapsulates such a crucial transition.

Later long barrows could be far more massive, and their characteristic form might be rendered in a more durable medium through the building of cairns. This may have been what happened through time, so that the most impressive of these monuments were not the *direct* successors of long houses at all, but monuments that were constructed many generations later and in a completely different cultural setting. Their structural development had a logic of its own – a logic that may have varied from one part of Europe to another – but what matters here is their original source of inspiration. They seem to have been explicitly designed as the houses of the dead, yet after the first of these monuments had been constructed they were also versions of *the dwellings of the past*. Long houses were not built again in prehistoric Europe until the construction and use of these sites had run its course.

It may have been important, then, that the houses of the dead should refer back to a prototype that was no longer being built. This is a significant point since the chronological distance between these structures and the latest long houses has been thought to weaken this argument (Scarre 1998). That is because the critics have not considered the importance of origin myths in traditional societies. In fact the long mounds and long cairns extend across a rather shorter period of time than the collection and deposition of Spondylus shells in Neolithic Europe. It may have been precisely because the long houses were so far beyond recall that the tradition of commemorating them by monuments assumed so great a significance.

The use of these particular monuments ran in parallel with the construction of an even more widely distributed form of earthwork: the causewayed enclosure. Again this may have originated in North-West Europe (Bradley 1998: chapter 5). The first earthwork enclosures seem to have been associated with the late Linearbandkeramik. Some of them may have surrounded groups of houses while at other sites they were not created until a settlement had been abandoned. They have also been interpreted as defences (Keeley and Cahen 1987), although the evidence for this suggestion is not particularly convincing.

The first of these enclosures were very different from the later generations of earthworks, for they were usually quite small and were defined by a continuous perimeter. It was mostly the later enclosures that were defined by segmented ditches. A few of these sites were still associated with long houses, in particular a number of examples close to the agricultural frontier in Belgium (ibid.), but a growing proportion of the causewayed enclosures seems to have formed a self-contained class of monument, quite distinct from the occupation sites of the same period. They provide increasing evidence of ritual activity, including human burials, large numbers of animal bones, pits containing carefully placed deposits, and finds of exotic artefacts. It was in this form that the distribution of these monuments expanded to reach its farthest limits in Denmark, Sweden, Britain, Ireland and Western France (Bradley 1998: chapter 5).

Just as the long barrow could be interpreted as making a reference to the practice of building long houses, the causewayed enclosure may be seen as a symbolic reference to the settlement as a whole. Both kinds of monument can be found close together, but not in every region, yet there may be another connection between these two ways of commemorating the past. One of the most distinctive features of the long house was the organisation of the borrow pits. These did have a practical function in supplying material for the walls, but they also seem to have been located so as to emphasise the divisions inside these buildings. In a few cases those divisions were also marked by burials. Perhaps the segmented boundaries around individual long houses have been considered in an excessively functional light. Could it be that by defining an entire enclosure in a similar manner the people who built it were suggesting that this particular space was equivalent to a settlement in the past?

The argument is circumstantial but it parallels my interpretation of the origins of long barrows. Both kinds of earthwork monument were built in parts of Europe that saw little sign of Neolithic activity until 4000 BC, or a little earlier. This is to say, they are regions in which long houses and enclosed settlements had played little or no part. When domesticated resources started to be used there, this happened in a very different setting. Occupation sites can be more difficult to discover and some of the buildings associated with them are surprisingly insubstantial. Yet in these very same landscapes we find a series of monuments that seem like the ghosts of an older way of living (Figure 2.7). There are representations of the long house and models of the enclosed settlement, but the long houses are represented by earthworks and cover the remains of the dead, while the enclosures are empty of buildings and associated with deposits of cultural material which stand out from the normal domestic assemblage. These were *landscapes of memory*, whose characteristic form recalled an ideal existence that had been followed in the remote past. More than that, there may be cases in which that traditional way of life had actually been followed *in a geographically distant area*. It is as if the outlines of an archaic settlement pattern were perpetuated in a purely symbolic form. These monuments presented an idealised conception of a world that had slipped beyond the bounds of history and was receding into myth.

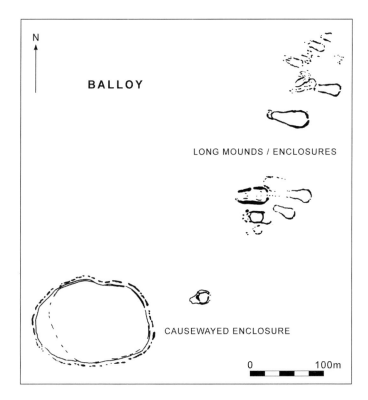

Figure 2.7 The distribution of long barrows at Balloy, Northern France, in relation to the position of a nearby causewayed enclosure.

Source: information from Mordant (1998).

Again there is a striking paradox to consider. The houses of the Linearband-keramik were massive structures, but in another sense they were also ephemeral, for after a relatively short period, perhaps a generation, they were abandoned and left to decay. In the same way, the settlements of which they formed a part might be used over a significant period of time, but then they too were abandoned, in some cases before the development of individual houses had run its course. Like those buildings, their positions were often avoided by later sites, so that they appeared as gaps in an increasingly populous landscape. The same is apparently true of the earliest enclosures.

The later earthworks provide a complete contrast. They were built in a form that was intended to leave a visible mark. Some of them were carefully maintained over a long period of time, and they were not levelled or significantly damaged within the Neolithic. In short, these constructions were meant to be remembered. They intruded on the consciousness of later generations whether or not anyone would have understood their meaning. However these features were interpreted, they could not be ignored. It was one way in which prehistoric people may have been able to create some sense of their own past, just as archaeologists can use the very same material to construct a past for themselves. The origin myths of the Neolithic and the conjectures of modern scholars could be very different from one another, but they share the same point of departure.

That was not the only course through which memory could be channelled.

Architects in contention

It was towards the western rim of the continent that the tradition of long mounds and long houses underwent its final transformation. On the coastline of North-West France there are oval and rectangular mounds (*tertres tumulaires*) that seem to have been built towards the beginning of the Neolithic (Boujot and Cassen 1993 and 1998). Round mounds are also found there and the burials that are associated with all three kinds of monument have a distinctive character. While they can be associated with a range of striking grave goods, including polished axe heads, they are contained within small stone settings or *cists* which were entirely inaccessible after those mounds had been constructed. The number of separate deposits might vary from site to site but what is clear is that the covering earthwork cut them off from the living population. Although no trace of the bodies or the associated artefacts remained, there is evidence that at some sites standing stones had been erected beside these monuments.

That suggests a subtle contrast between the nature of the burial, which removed the remains of the dead from view, and the erection of *menhirs* which commemorated the past in a way that might still be visible (Bradley 1998: chapter 4). It is not clear whether the menhirs were intended to represent individual people or divinities, but the surviving decoration contains a series of arcane images, including artefacts and animals. Whittle (2000) has suggested that these may have had a mythological significance, charting the origins of the local population and its place in the world.

In the same region of Europe, the tradition of building long mounds came into contact with another architectural style known as the passage grave. The relationship between the two kinds of monument is controversial and it still remains to be established how far they co-existed (Scarre 1992 and 1998). Much of the discussion has been concerned with typology, but the most important difference between these kinds of monument involves the ways in which they could be used (Figure 2.8).

As the name suggests, passage graves established a direct connection between a burial chamber (the 'grave') and the outside world. For that reason they could have been used over a lengthy period and people would have been able to visit the remains of the dead for a long time after they were deposited (Bradley 1998: chapter 4). Certain of these tombs were also decorated, and the placing of the different motifs might have played a part in the ceremonies that were conducted there.

In North-West France it has always been difficult to establish the chrono-logical relationship between these different kinds of monument, and so much attention has been paid to problems of sequence that the broader significance of these constructions can easily be overlooked. Some points are well established. A number of the long mounds that covered inaccessible burials were later converted into passage graves. Perhaps the clearest sequence of this kind was

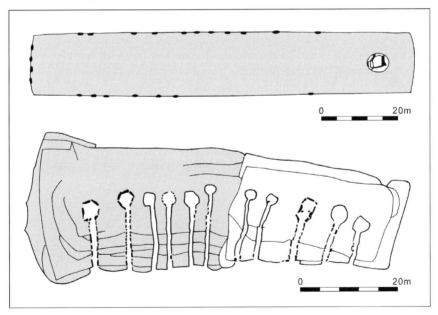

Figure 2.8 Contrasts in the organisation of space in the early long mounds or long cairns of North-West France. The upper plan shows the tertre tumulaire at Kerlud, Brittany, and the lower plan the two-phase monument at Barnenez, Finistère.

Sources: information from Giot (1987) and Boujot and Cassen (1998).

established at Le Petit Mont, Arzon (Lecornec 1994), but, since that site was excavated, similar evidence has been identified elsewhere in Brittany (Cassen 2000). In such cases, passage graves were built at the edge of the original structure, or the primary long mound was incorporated within a larger monument containing one or more tombs of this kind. There are other structures in which an elongated cairn might contain a whole series of separate chambers. The best known example of this arrangement is at Barnenez in Finistère (Giot 1987, volume 1: 3–102). Clearly these sites involved a combination of structural features that might otherwise appear in separate contexts. Any one site could draw on architectural elements taken from different traditions, so that the finished form of these monuments resulted from a kind of *bricolage*.

That is certainly the case if the evidence is viewed at a larger scale. Passage graves are distributed along the Atlantic coastline from Portugal to Brittany, with other, generally later groups in the West Mediterranean, Ireland, Britain, North Germany and South Scandinavia. The oldest examples may be those in Western France and Southern Portugal, which seem to date from the mid fifth millennium BC (Scarre, Switsur and Mohen 1993; Giot, Marguerie and Morzadec 1994; Müller 1999). Some of the first passage graves in these areas were associated with circular mounds and cairns. This contrasts with the history of long barrows which originated further to the east.

Because of the distinctive distribution of early passage graves, it has always been tempting to connect their origins with the late Mesolithic population of Atlantic Europe and with the formative phase in the adoption of agriculture associated with Cardial Ware and its derivatives. Their distribution is now known to extend from the Mediterranean, through parts of Iberia into Western France. It is certainly true that within this broad geographical area there are precedents for Mesolithic burials associated with grave goods and with rudimentary stone constructions (Scarre 1992). Indeed, Sherratt (1990) has even argued that the passage graves associated with circular cairns may have enshrined the idea of a Mesolithic round house just as the long mounds found in North-West Europe may have been influenced by the domestic buildings of the Linearbandkeramik.

The statues that moved

Another element in this process is the use and reuse of menhirs, whose distribution in Southern Brittany resembles that of tertres tumulaires (Boujot and Cassen 1998). It has long been recognised that a number of passage graves in North-West France were decorated with pecked motifs. Although the monuments themselves had been poorly excavated, it was first observed in the nineteenth century that many of these carved stones were not in their original contexts. A number of the monuments were reusing decorated menhirs, some of which remained intact while others were broken (Cassen 2000). Two recent developments have been especially revealing. Excavation of the chambered tomb at Gavrinis revealed that part of a decorated stone had been incorporated into the roof of the chamber, while a joining fragment had been reused in a passage grave, La Table des Marchand, three kilometres away (Figure 2.9) (Le Roux 1984). This could be shown because the same decorative scheme had continued across both these fragments. Not long afterwards, excavation close to the latter site identified the sockets for a substantial alignment of other menhirs terminating at Le Grand Menhir Brisé, the largest standing stone in Brittany. Although this monolith had been felled, it still remained close to its original position, whereas the other menhirs had all been taken away (Figure 2.10). It seems likely that one of them included the decorated pieces just described (L'Helgouac'h 1999).

There is a complex interplay between these different elements in the pre-history of North-West France. Some of the decorated menhirs remained in position, but at Locmariaquer, where it seems as if the stone row had accom-panied a long mound, the individual components were uprooted; fragments of these monoliths may have been distributed among local passage graves (L'Helgouac'h 1999). In the same way, at Le Petit Mont, Arzon, it seems as if at least one such menhir had been erected at the end of another early long mound (Lecornec 1994). As so often, it had been removed and could have been incor-porated in the tomb that took its place. Again that structure included numerous fragments of already carved stone.

There were at least two possible relationships between the standing stones and

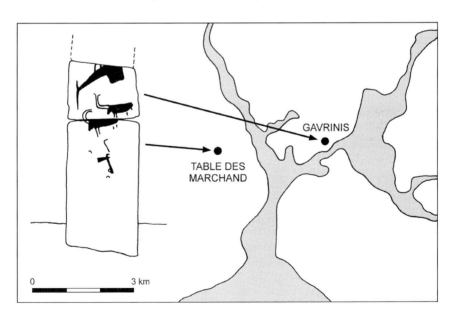

Figure 2.9 The reuse of carved stones in chambered tombs near Locmariaquer, Brittany.
Source: information from Whittle (2000).

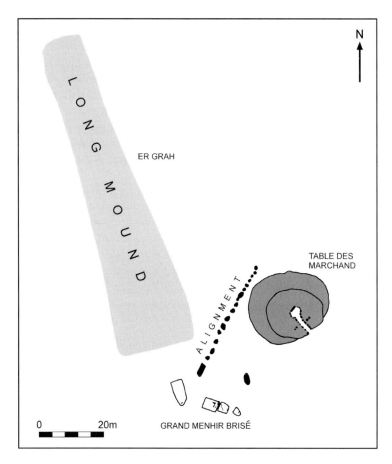

Figure 2.10 A long mound (Er Grah), a passage grave (Table des Marchand) and a
          stone alignment at Locmariaquer, Brittany.

Source: information from L'Helgouac'h (1999).

megalithic tombs in this area. In a few cases it seems as if menhirs stood upright
inside the chambers themselves, as happened at Barnenez (Giot 1987), although
it is difficult to say whether they had been brought there from other sites. At all
events, they were now concealed from view. In other cases menhirs were taken
down and sometimes reduced to fragments before they were built into the fabric
of chambered tombs. In at least one instance it is clear that pieces of a single stone
were distributed between different monuments. It is uncertain how long this
process might have taken.

For many scholars the treatment of these menhirs amounts to iconoclasm
(Cassen 2000; Whittle 2000). Stones which had an established meaning in the
landscape were taken down and sometimes destroyed. Some of them were

associated with long mounds, and the change appears to have happened when passage graves were built. For that reason the sequence might have resulted from the conflict between two different systems of belief. Either the builders of the chambered tombs desecrated existing sacred places, levelling them to the ground and removing their remains, or they took them over but transferred the established significance of the decorated stones to a different kind of monument.

The imagery on these stones is most distinctive. In addition to purely abstract devices, it contains a number of elements that might refer to the changes that took place at the beginning of the Neolithic period. These include drawings of artefacts (axe heads, bows and arrows) and images of domestic animals. They may also include depictions of whales. A literal reading of these symbols would emphasise the mixture of hunting, fishing and stock raising that might be expected at this time. Whittle (2000) has considered whether these were the work of an indigenous population that was coming to terms with a new way of life. Cassen (2000), on the other hand, suggests that the archaeological sequence involves a major change in the gender associations of the monuments.

The details of these different interpretations are less important than their consequences, for one possibility is that by levelling the decorated stones and distributing their remains between a number of chambered tombs, people were rejecting established ideas about the world. In one version of that argument, images that could have been related to a distant past were replaced by a new form of monument and the beliefs with which it was associated. In place of memorials to that past, there came an enforced forgetting.

Those interpretations could well encapsulate the archaeological sequence in Brittany where two quite different approaches to commemorating the dead came into contact, but it would not work so well if similar processes had extended far beyond this particular region. *That is exactly what we find.* Recent work in Spain and Portugal has provided some striking evidence of similar practices, extending from the Atlantic into the West Mediterranean (Bueno Ramirez and de Balbín Behrmann 1997 and 2000).

This evidence takes two forms. First, it has become clear that decorated menhirs are widely distributed across the Iberian peninsula and that a number of them were embellished with similar motifs to those in France, in particular the serpent and the crook. These are found over a large area but the similarities are sufficiently striking to suggest direct links between them. That is especially important as carvings of crooks are associated with a series of stone settings in the Alentejo, Southern Portugal, which have been attributed to the beginning of the Neolithic period (Calado 1997). One reason for emphasising this point is that these particular sites bear a marked resemblance to the enclosures known as *cromlechs* in North-West France.

The second reason for reconsidering the accepted interpretation of the Breton sequence is the occurrence of menhirs inside Iberian megalithic tombs. In recent years this has been the subject of a systematic investigation by Bueno Ramirez and de Balbín Behrmann (1997 and 2000). Several of their findings recall the evidence from Northern France (Figure 2.11). Decorated menhirs can be identified in close proximity to groups of megaliths, and in certain cases similar pieces have been recognised as free-standing elements within these structures. More frequently, the fabric of the tombs themselves includes large fragments of decorated stone, which were probably moved there from another location. These were not distributed at random, and most of them are found at the back of these structures and around the junction between the chamber and the passage.

This suggests that a more general process could lie behind the sequence in

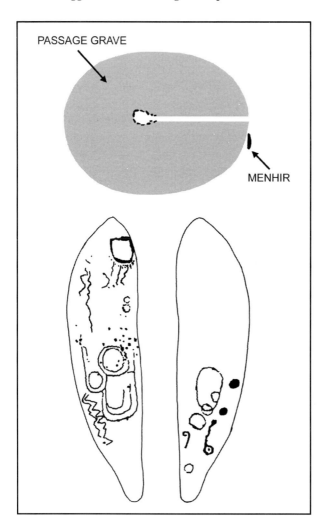

Figure 2.11 Decorated menhir and passage grave at Vale de Rodrigo, Alentejo, Portugal.

Source: information from Bueno Ramirez and de Balbín Behrmann (2000).

North-West France. In Brittany, it is perfectly plausible to see the distinctive archaeological sequence as a result of the gradual playing out of political and ideological relationships between an indigenous population and groups of settlers from the east. Although the adoption of agriculture in Iberia may also have involved the movement of people, the two situations are hardly similar to one another, yet the archaeology of these areas has some of the same elements in common: the raising of decorated menhirs in the open air and their eventual incorporation within the fabric of chambered tombs. Perhaps these specific elements were more closely related than has seemed apparent. If so, then it is necessary to look for an explanation that fits the evidence *from both regions*.

The implications of malangan

We can compare this process with a sequence described by Küchler (1987 and 1999) in an account of mortuary ritual in New Ireland. Here we encounter a case in which memory was created through the loss of material culture.

> Malangan . . . designates a ritual performance centred around the construction of architectural structures which become the site for the display of effigies, songs and dances, commemorative vessels for the transposition of life force after death. Often taking months to produce, malangan with all its ritual paraphernalia, is no more than a temporary abode to the soul of the dead. Upon destruction of its container, the soul becomes image and thus a mobile, floating memory. *The control over this memory is of paramount importance to the regulation of other forms of ownership in land or titles.*
>
> (1999: 64 [my emphasis])

One of the main ways in which this transition is effected is through the production of effigies, which come to stand for the dead and their importance in society. As Gell puts it,

> all the dispersed 'social effectiveness' of the deceased, the difference they made to how things were, gradually becomes an objectifiable quantity, something to which a single material index may be attached and from which this accumulated effectiveness may be abducted. That is what the Malangan is: a kind of body which accumulates, like a charged battery, the potential energy of the deceased dispersed in the life-world.
>
> (1998: 225)

Malangan can be made out of wood or vines and is sometimes large and elaborate. It assumes a most distinctive form:

> Visually and conceptually, [it] recall[s] a body wrapped in images. . . . Incised to the point of breakage, the emerging fretwork takes the form of instantly

> recognisable motifs found in abundance in the physical and animate
> environment of the island culture that produced them.
>
> (Küchler 1999: 56)

These images are allowed to decay in parallel with the remains of the dead and,
when the physical residues of mourning decompose, what is left is a memory of
the creation and display of what Küchler calls the 'figure-corpse'. Its condition
mirrors the treatment of the dead, and in the end no trace of either survives.
Instead of a permanent memorial, the dissolution of the image provides a vivid
metaphor for the decay of the human body, and it is this process that is called to
mind. By destroying an object which has achieved renown it is possible to ensure
that it will form part of public tradition. This is a classic example of 'remembering
by forgetting'.

Remembering by forgetting

Perhaps this process is comparable with the evidence of the Neolithic menhirs.
The analogy can be considered on several different levels. There is the largely
anecdotal similarity between the malangan adorned with images drawn from the
local environment and the menhirs found in Neolithic Brittany, which have a
rather similar repertoire illustrating some of the principal animals and objects
encountered in daily life. Again it seems quite possible that these provided a kind
of summary of the roles or achievements of the deceased, or of remoter figures
from whom they claimed descent.

A second comparison concerns the treatment of these images in prehistory.
They were erected in the open air, in some cases close to monuments, and yet
after an interval of uncertain duration many of them were levelled and reduced to
fragments. The decorated image may have taken on the function of the corpse.
This is clear from the Melanesian example, but it is also implicit in the use of
passage graves, rather than the long barrows that they sometimes replaced. A
decorated menhir associated with one of those early sites might have been
modified or removed, but its treatment could not be assimilated to that of the
deceased because the cists beneath the mound were inaccessible. The adoption of
passage graves changed that relationship entirely, and it is surely the reason why
their fabric incorporates so many pieces of reused stonework.

I have suggested that one of the roles of the passage grave was to ensure
continuous contact between the living and the dead. That would have permitted
the addition, rearrangement and removal of bones. It may also have led to a
gradual merging of individual identities so that the remains of different people
became mixed together in a variety of formal patterns that extended throughout
the monument. The use of these particular tombs created a community of the
dead out of the physical remains of a number of separate people; few bones
survive in the Breton monuments, but this interpretation is supported by
excavations in Northern France (Patton 1993: 91–8).

The reuse of menhirs may have been a rather similar process. Because of their close association with the early mounds, these seem to have been intended as memorials to the dead, although this may not have been their only role. In time they were translated from the outside world into the monument, in the same way as human remains were introduced to these sites. The sculpted fragments were concealed in the structure of the tombs just like the relics of the dead, and now it seems possible that these monuments brought together fragments from different standing stones, so that their separate identities were merged in the same manner as the human remains. Again I must emphasise that we do not know how long the menhirs had stood in the open air before this happened.

Like the distinctive images described by Küchler in New Ireland, the menhirs that were built into passage graves may result from a quite distinctive process in which the destruction and concealment of decorated stones was a way of fixing social memories. Over a period of time that would be just as effective as the preservation and maintenance of memorials in the wider landscape. But in this case there is one vital difference, for the passage graves themselves were major monuments. On an individual level, the destruction of Neolithic menhirs may have helped to fix the memories of particular people in the past, while at a public level the tombs in which fragments of these statues were embedded celebrated the continuity of a larger social group. This process may well have been one by which the dead were finally categorised as ancestors. Over time those practices might have contributed to another kind of origin myth (for a similar interpretation of the rock art of Valcamonica, published after this chapter was written, see Keates 2000).

This might seem to be a tenuous interpretation, depending on comparison with a single ethnographic example, but that is not the case. Standing stones in the form of *stelai* and statue menhirs are widely distributed in prehistory. In addition to those mentioned already, they occur close to the Black Sea, on several of the Mediterranean islands, in Northern Germany, Southern France, in the Alps and in Ireland (Mezzena 1998a). Their chronological distribution is equally varied, and examples are known from the later phases of the Neolithic period, the Copper Age and throughout the Bronze Age. Examples have even been found in association with Hallstatt tumuli. Although some scholars have looked for a single origin, usually in South-East Europe, these stone sculptures are too widely distributed across time and space for this to be particularly likely (Barfield 1995; Mallory 1995). Since many of them depict the human body, albeit in a highly stylised manner, there seems no reason to look for a single prototype in antiquity.

Despite the wide distribution of these images, there are few in primary contexts: a large number of the statues have been reused. We must be wary of taking this evidence too literally as examples in the open air will often have been damaged or removed, yet it is extraordinary how often they are found as fragments in mortuary monuments. Apart from the examples already quoted from the Neolithic of Atlantic Europe, this happened in the late Neolithic/Copper Age in the southern Alps and in the same period in Northern Germany. In the

Early Bronze Age there is similar evidence from regions as far apart as Iberia and the Black Sea (Mezzena 1998a).

At times the evidence takes a very similar form even in areas that are unlikely to have been in contact with one another. Thus dismantled statues or relief sculptures are associated with human burials in the Maikop Culture of South-East Europe and in the decorated cists of Southern Portugal. In the same way, the remains of statues are found in some of the earliest megalithic tombs in Atlantic Europe and in the latest examples in the Swiss Alps. The imagery associated with these sites has little or nothing in common and these monuments are separated in time by over 1000 years, yet the ways in which they were used are strikingly similar to one another (ibid.).

Petit Chasseur

This is well illustrated by a site at Sion in the southern Alps where part of a major cemetery, Petit Chasseur, has been excavated. This work had several advantages over the projects described so far. The site had a detailed stratigraphic sequence, the carved stones were so well preserved that it was possible to study their individual histories in detail, human bones still survived, and the interpretation of the site is supported by a series of radiocarbon dates (Gallay 1995).

Petit Chasseur has a complex history, only the earlier stages of which are relevant at this point (Table 2.1); the sequence will be considered again in Chapter 4. Between about 2900 and 2700 BC a megalithic tomb was built, and it was followed not long afterwards by a second monument of the same type.

Table 2.1 The archaeological sequence at Petit Chasseur

Date (BC)	Type of monument	Mode of burial	Erection of menhirs	Reuse of Type A menhirs	Reuse of Type B menhirs
2900	Megalith	Collective	–	–	–
	Megalith	Collective	+	×	–
2450	Cist	Collective	+	×	×
	Cist	Single and collective	+	–	×
2100	Cairn	Single and secondary cremation	+	–	×
	Cairn	Single and secondary cremation	–	–	–

Source: information from Gallay (1995).

Notes
+ Indicates the presence of evidence in each phase.
– Indicates that evidence is absent.
× Indicates the contexts in which older menhirs were reused.

Both comprised accessible stone-built chambers which projected above the low triangular cairns or platforms that encased them. Each tomb was associated with the remains of collective burials, and the later of these monuments seems to have had two statue menhirs flanking its entrance. Others may have existed in the vicinity, as fragments of several more were reused in the burials of the following phase. These early sculptures represented the outline of a human body. Sometimes it was accompanied by a spiral ornament and at least one dagger (Figure 2.12).

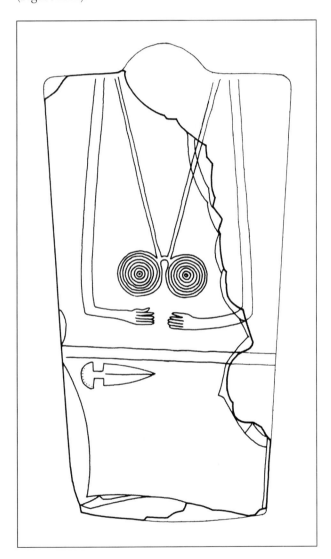

Figure 2.12 A damaged statue menhir from Petit Chasseur, Switzerland.

Not long afterwards, around 2400 BC, a further series of monuments was erected, but this time they took the form of massive cists, one of which was enclosed by a setting of posts. Again the chambers were associated with multiple burials, but this time they contained Bell Beaker pottery. These monuments had a new feature, for their construction reused fragments of older carvings. The excavator suggests that during the same phase one of the burial deposits in an earlier tomb was disturbed. The human bones were removed from the chamber and new burials, again associated with Beakers, took their place. Although he considers this as a 'violation' of the older monument, he records that some of these bones had been rearranged, so that the skulls were carefully aligned along the edge of the existing platform.

These changes continued into subsequent phases with the creation of rather smaller cists, each of them containing the remains of one or more individuals. They had the same ceramic association and again these monuments had been built out of the remains of statues. The difference is that they were carved in another style. Now they were more richly decorated and seemed to show elaborate costumes. The daggers found in the older sculptures had been replaced by bows and arrows. In a subsequent phase, provisionally dated to about 2100 BC, further fragments of the same kind were reused in building small altars in front of the existing tombs.

For most of this time it seems as if statue menhirs were being made and erected outside individual monuments before they were taken down; some of their original sockets could be identified by excavation. The fragments were then incorporated into a variety of different monuments, from a megalithic tomb associated with a long triangular platform to successive generations of cists, most of which were associated with collective burials and Beaker pottery. The excavator regards this as a continuous process, for the style of the reused carvings changed in parallel with the sequence of monuments.

Interpretations of this phenomenon have changed over the years. At first the excavator envisaged a major break in the sequence, marked by the settlement of people who made Beaker pottery. They desecrated an existing megalith and removed its contents, before they took over the monument for burials of their own. They also broke a series of sculptured stones and employed them in building cists. That hypothesis recalls interpretations of the sequence in Breton tombs, but it seems inconsistent with the pattern of use and reuse shown by the statues at Petit Chasseur. They were employed continuously from the Late Neolithic period through the Early Bronze Age and studies of the skeletal material from the site have not suggested any change of population during that time. Rather, it seems as if the history of the site followed a ritual cycle that was largely unaffected by the changing forms and associations of the monuments. Stone chambers of various types were linked with the creation of stone statues, which originally stood in the open air. After an unknown interval, these statues were taken down, often with some violence, and they were broken up to varying degrees. A number of examples show more than one phase of decoration and an interesting feature is that so many of them seem to have been decapitated. It may have been when this happened that their remains were built into the tombs.

Very similar rituals seem to have been followed at sites of quite different dates and affiliations. It suggests that cycles of this kind were being followed in many regions and that the resemblance between them calls for a single explanation. I have suggested one possibility here, but it can only be assessed in any detail when more dating evidence becomes available.

A summary

This chapter has considered two case studies from the early Neolithic settlement of Western Europe. These have been concerned with each of the principal axes that have been identified during this period. One extended from the Balkans through the Rhineland towards the Channel coast, while the other connected the West Mediterranean to the Atlantic seaboard. Each began with one of the main ceramic traditions of the Neolithic period: the Linearbandkeramik and Cardial Ware, respectively.

What these examples have in common is a shared emphasis on the past, which would have been particularly appropriate during a period in which new regions were settled and new relationships were formed between people and the land. In one case this was achieved by emphasising a myth of distant origins, which was translated from the medium of house-building to the creation of earthworks dedicated to the dead. That connection gained added emphasis from the movement of seashells originating in Southern Europe. It was initially established through the orientations of settlements and graves, but in its later manifestation it was enshrined in the structure of considerable monuments. In that case social memories were transmitted to later generations in a seemingly permanent form.

Along the Atlantic seaboard there were other monuments, but the ways in which they were used were rather different, for this region seems to have been characterised by a series of stone statues that were evidently associated with the dead. Whether they were regarded as memorials to individuals it is hard to say, although there may be analogies for this practice from other periods and other regions. Whatever the solution, it is clear that many of these standing stones had a limited life span, despite the considerable amount of labour involved in their creation. That is because they were eventually overthrown. The fragments were then reused in the fabric of the tombs, where their remains were effectively concealed. Indeed, it seems quite possible that the use of individual statues in the chambered tombs followed the same procedures as the treatment of bodies on these sites. In this case it was the act of destroying these statues and removing them from view that was the main source of human memory, and it could have been through creating traditions in this way that the achievements of particular individuals might have been recalled.

Both these processes are concerned with the celebration and codification of origins, but they took very different courses from one region to another. To some extent that is because they represent two quite distinct ways of thinking about the past, but, even so, they do have one important feature in common. Both show how people in prehistoric Europe were concerned with their beginnings in more distant places and times. As we shall see in Chapter 3, similar concerns would also extend to their attitude to the immediate past and to its relationship with the present.

Chapter 3

Entering the present
Legacies of the immediate past

Lifelines

At the end of his life the Italian writer Calvino prepared a series of lectures on the qualities that would be needed in the literature of the new millennium (Calvino 1992). One of them was 'quickness'. He illustrates his point with the story of a magic ring. I quote his comments here because they could have been written by an archaeologist:

> The real protagonist of the story . . . is the ring, because it is the movements of the ring that determine those of the characters and because it is the ring that establishes the relationships between them. Around the magic object there forms a kind of force field that is the territory of the story itself. We might say that the magic object is the outward and visible sign that reveals the connection between people or between events. It has a narrative function . . . that continues to surface in the Renaissance. In Ariosto's *Orlando furioso* we find an endless series of exchanges of swords, shields, helmets and horses, each one endowed with particular qualities. *In this way the plot can be described in terms of the changes of ownership of a certain number of objects, each one endowed with certain powers that determine the relationships between certain characters.*
>
> (1992: 32–3 [my emphasis])

In this version artefacts have histories like those of human beings, and objects play an active part in the narrative. *Orlando furioso* is an epic poem like the *Aeneid*, the *Iliad* and the *Odyssey*, and it fulfilled a similar function. It was published by Ariosto in 1532 and was composed to celebrate the house of Este and its legendary ancestor Rogero. On that level it refers back to a distant origin. At the same time, Calvino makes it clear that the narrative derives much of its impetus from the continuous projection of the past into the present through the exchange of artefacts. These particular transactions were the prerogative of an elite, but the same principle applies to more mundane objects as well. A good example might be coins.

The most familiar way of teaching archaeological dating is to examine the money in one's pocket. I tried the experiment myself on starting to write this chapter. In my own case a small selection of change yielded dates extending from 1977 up to the year 2000. The distribution of dates was weighted towards the mid 1980s, and yet these words are written nearly 15 years later. The underlying principle is a simple one: coins can be used to suggest a minimum age for whatever event is being studied, and the last to be issued offers the least unreliable estimate.

That has been a principle of archaeology since the early years of the discipline and yet this argument side-steps other interesting issues. Like the weapons mentioned by Calvino, each of the coins had its own history from the day that it was issued. These particular coins are most unlikely to have been brought together in the same combination before, and in future they will go their separate ways again. They may have been employed in many kinds of transaction in the past, but their use will also continue until particular denominations are recalled. By that time some of them will probably have been lost. A small sample may even be retained as collectors' items, in which case their worth will be reckoned according to a different scale of value from the other coins.

The same principles apply to the material environment in which people live. I am writing these words in a house that was built more than 100 years ago, although it has been changed since then. Most of the rooms have their own locks and keys because at one stage it seems to have been occupied by paying guests. On the wall in front of me there are paintings whose history spans five decades. The books on the shelves extend back to the nineteenth century, and outside the window are two apple trees which are the only survivors of an orchard that was there before the house was built. As an archaeologist, I also have a few antiquities in my room: a Neolithic axe, a fragment of a Medieval stone carving and some of the artefacts from a recent excavation.

Not surprisingly, I can recall where and when I acquired these items, and in that sense they have made themselves part of my life history. I know that one picture was a present, that certain books were acquired to help with a particular piece of research and that some of the novels describe places I have visited. But each of these objects has its history, too. My copy of William Greenwell's *British Barrows*, for instance, bears the signatures of its previous owners, from J. R. Mortimer to A. L. F Rivet. A book by General Pitt Rivers was signed by the author and had circulated for 90 years before it came to me.

There is nothing remarkable about this process, which is part of everyone's experience. It is the very fact that it is universal that makes it so important for archaeologists to understand its implications. Ever since Appadurai's edited volume, *The Social Life of Things*, appeared in 1986, prehistorians have tried to study the 'cultural biographies' of artefacts and monuments. The term refers to the various ways in which those 'things' had been treated between their creation and their destruction (although, strictly speaking, their stories start again as soon as they become the object of study). As Calvino shows, artefacts have their biographies just as people do. Their use at any one point involves the intersection of many separate time scales: the periods over which these items have already been used, and the various processes they have still to undergo.

The point is well put by Olivier:

> Living things, such as systems and beings, are continuously evolving but they simultaneously remain what they are, since, through growth, every stage of their transformation is recorded in matter. In other words, evolutionary processes simultaneously follow two opposite directions: one points towards the future (by transforming), while the other goes back towards the past (by ageing), that is to say, by constantly preserving a record of the present. The arrow of time is concurrently flying towards opposite targets, that of the future and that of the past. Here, matter plays a crucial role, since it is the medium of *memory:* it is this basic property of matter constantly to record the present that allows . . . the existence of archaeology.
>
> (1999: 531 [emphasis in the original])

There is a risk that the current emphasis on 'the cultural biographies of things' may lose sight of the fact that their main relevance to prehistoric archaeology concerns the ways in which such life histories cut across those of *particular human beings*. That may be only a brief episode in the biography of any one object, yet that encounter can have important consequences. A recent study by Hoskins (1998) makes this point. Hoskins carried out ethnographic research in eastern Indonesia and as part of her project she wished to learn more about the individuals she was studying. She found it difficult to persuade them to tell their stories. That is very unlike the situation in the modern West and it posed a problem for her work:

> The notion of telling one's life directly to another person did not exist in Kodi. From men, especially prominent ones, I often heard a list of accomplishments, offices or ceremonies performed. From women, the question 'Tell me about your life' usually initially produced little more than a list of children. But I did get some insight into personal experience and subjective reactions through a set of interviews that I was conducting on another topic – the history of exchange objects and of ritually important domestic objects.
>
> What I discovered, quite to my surprise, was that I could not collect the histories of objects and the life histories of persons separately. People and the things they valued were so completely intertwined they could not be disentangled. The frustration I experienced in trying to follow my planned methodology proved to be an advantage in disguise. I obtained more introspective, intimate, and 'personal' accounts of many peoples' lives when I asked them about objects, and traced the path of many objects in interviews supposedly focused on persons.
>
> (1998: 2)

People may think about their lives in relation to the artefacts they encounter at different times. In fact those objects may become part of their life stories, whether or not it is considered appropriate for individuals to talk about themselves. What Hoskins calls 'biographical objects' provide an important way of bringing the past to bear on the present: they are among the sources out of which histories are made. At the same time, the careers of such artefacts may be largely independent of specific individuals, intervening in their experiences only briefly before they go on to touch other lives. Any collection of material culture, such as those studied by archaeologists, may be a temporary accumulation of artefacts which stand in various quite different relations to the passage of time. That is how I can work in a room which contains prehistoric artefacts, new novels and nineteenth century monographs. Each of these has followed a very different trajectory and, no doubt, will continue to do so in the future.

What applies on an individual level applies on a larger scale as well. Again this has implications for archaeological practice. Prehistorians investigate an unbroken span of time, but in order to come to terms with their material they organise it into chronological periods. This was one of the first procedures developed in the nineteenth century, and it has provided a means by which individual researchers identify themselves and the work they do. One person may be a Neolithic specialist; another may specialise on the Iron Age. It also influences the ways in which they write, so that the events that preceded their period of interest are relegated to a 'background' and are not given the same weight as the main subject matter. This is unavoidable, for the only other option is to trace every archaeological narrative back to the genesis of Homo Sapiens, but it does run the risk of being unintentionally misleading. What tends to be forgotten is that the earlier 'background' to the field of study was often the visible world which people inherited from the past and in which they lived. They would not have had the option of restarting their lives according to the period divisions in a textbook they would never see.

Barrett (1999) makes this point in an account of the Iron Age mythological landscape of Southern England. At first sight one might suppose that it could be studied by considering those cases in which existing structures or features of the topography were modified during this period. Barrett does not take this course. For him, that mythological landscape consists of the prominent earthworks of much older burial mounds. They did not date from the recent past and few, if any, of these were used during the Iron Age itself. But they would have been inescapable features of the land that people inhabited and it would have been necessary to come to terms with them even if their surviving fabric was shunned:

> The world as it already existed will always have been imbued with meanings and have been used as a background of reference against which contemporary acts . . . were played out. Indeed, these acts may often have sought to make explicit the meanings which were soaked into the landscape, or to find ways to focus them more directly upon contemporary concerns. . . . The

modification of the landscape lay not so much in its physical modification as in its interpretation. . . .

The past, necessarily absent, must none the less have been represented by the relics of the earlier period, perhaps most evocatively by the burial mounds themselves. Burials no longer took place in or even around these mounds but this very lack of intervention best expresses the role the mounds now played. The mythical stood apart from the present. In its form the landscape contained the relics of those times occupying . . . the horizons beyond the routines of daily life.

(1999: 262)

It follows from this that prehistoric lives would always have been conducted according to an awareness of history, even if it could not be measured in the terms that are used today. That awareness would have extended from the origins and use of artefacts acquired in daily life, through the built fabric that ancient people inherited, to the wider landscapes in which they lived. The past was constantly caught up in the present, for this was where so many different time scales intersected. In the account that follows I shall consider this subject at three different scales. First, I shall discuss the roles played by artefacts, and the ways in which archaeologists have studied their deployment over time. Then the account shifts to settlement sites and develops some observations made in Chapter 2 about the building and replacement of houses. Finally, I shall discuss the ways in which people accommodated themselves to the surviving fabric of older prehistoric landscapes. For the most part the discussion will draw on evidence from the Netherlands, South Scandinavia and the British Isles.

Thinking about things

There is a problem in discussing the ways in which ancient artefacts were treated, for it is difficult to do so without flouting the principles of archaeological analysis. Put simply, the creation of a chronology depends on isolating what are described as 'closed groups': those collections of material which were deposited together on a single occasion. The usual examples are the contents of graves and hoards. It is by studying the entire network of such associations that it becomes possible to date specific artefact types. But there is a difficulty, for the method makes two assumptions that cannot always be justified. It assumes that no deposits were ever reopened for the addition of newer material, and it does not allow the possibility that the objects in these groups might have been of different ages from one another when they were brought together.

In certain cases the discrepancies are so obvious that these anomalies can be recognised. An obvious example is the presence of Early Bronze Age axes in a number of Middle and Late Bronze Age hoards. These stand out because they run counter to many other examples, but recently a series of still more unusual finds of metalwork has been identified in Southern England (Stead

1998: chapter 8). None is recorded in much detail, but they do share one feature in common. They consist of accumulations of artefacts, some of them buried in pits, whose individual components span an enormous period of time. Thus the Salisbury hoard contained over 500 artefacts, whose dates extend over at least 2000 years, from the earliest use of metal in Britain to the Late Iron Age. Another hoard included metalwork spanning a rather shorter period, from about 2000 to 300 BC, while the objects from the Danebury hoard were made at different times between about 1800 and 600 BC. That collection could have been buried when a hillfort was built on the site. Fortunately, its original context is known, but a similar group of metalwork from Hounslow shows just how difficult it is to recognise this phenomenon. Here a group of Bronze Age and Iron Age objects seems to have been found together, but when it was eventually acquired by the British Museum it was sorted into two separate 'hoards', on the premise that such material must have come from different deposits (ibid.).

It is hard to tell whether such anomalies were particularly common, although it is easy enough to quote individual instances from sites in Southern England. Among the more obvious examples are: two Mesolithic axes buried in a pit together with Iron Age pottery (Jon Cotton pers. comm.); a Neolithic axe head placed in the foundation trench for the rampart of a Bronze Age hillfort (Bradley and Ellison 1975: 86); and a Middle Bronze Age palstave that was apparently decorated with silver and placed in a Late Iron Age royal grave (Foster 1986: 78–80). The list could be much longer. In such cases the historical significance of particular objects would have been apparent, if only because they looked so different from the other artefacts on those sites. Their importance was emphasised by the ways in which they were deposited.

Calvino's summary of *Orlando furioso*, quoted at the beginning of this chapter, suggests another possibility, for it talks about 'an endless series of exchanges of swords, shields [and] helmets . . . each endowed with particular qualities'. The narrative, he tells us, 'can be described in terms of the changes of ownership of a certain number of objects, each one endowed with certain powers . . .' (1992: 33). In this case, the significance of such objects depends on their individual histories: on the people who had used them and the situations in which those artefacts were obtained. It is hard to translate this scheme into archaeological terms, because transactions of those kinds are virtually invisible. Prehistoric artefacts can only be observed when they have been taken out of circulation. On the other hand, the condition of those objects may provide indications of the ways in which they had been used; and sometimes that history helps us to interpret the contexts in which they are found.

Calvino refers to the exchange of weaponry, and this is particularly apposite as prehistoric examples can provide some relevant information. Two cases illustrate this point. In Denmark, Kristiansen (1984) has compared the biographies of different kinds of Early Bronze Age swords dating from Periods II and III. Flange-hilted swords seem to have been employed in combat and carry obvious traces of wear and resharpening, while the full-hilted swords show little sign that they had been used in the same way; instead they seem to have been largely ceremonial regalia. The distinction between these two types is reflected by their role in the burial rite, where each is associated with a rather different set of grave goods. For Kristiansen, the distinction is equivalent to that between warriors and chiefs.

A similar distinction is apparent among the weapons of Early Bronze Age Wessex, where Wall (1987) has examined a series of daggers for traces of use. Her conclusions are rather like Kristiansen's. Although there are two main series of daggers, dating from different phases, both show the same amounts of wear, and in each case there is evidence to suggest that they had been used over a significant period of time before they were committed to the ground. As some of these artefacts are finely formed and elaborately decorated, they may have been intended as insignia. By contrast, the simpler daggers that were made over the same period may have had shorter histories as there is significantly less wear on weapons of this kind (Table 3.1). For the most part they are found in the poorer burials of this period. In each of these examples, artefacts of broadly similar forms may have had different biographies, and this is reflected by their use in mortuary rites.

The burial of such weapons removed them from circulation but it did not entail any special kind of treatment. That was not the case with the metalwork of the Later Bronze Age that succeeded them. A recent study of the weapons deposited in the River Thames has shed some light on the complexity of this process (York 2002). Different weapons had been treated in different ways before they were placed in the river; swords and spears had their own histories from one period to another; a changing proportion of this material had been deliberately damaged; and these artefacts had been used to varying extents before they entered the water.

We can summarise the results of this analysis by considering the choices that had to be made in the past (Table 3.2). Once individual weapons had been produced – a process of which we have little knowledge until the Middle Bronze

Table 3.1 Wear and damage on Early Bronze Age daggers in Wessex

	Wessex 1/2 daggers	Wessex/non-Wessex daggers
Survival of rivets	*	**
Re-sharpening of blade	–	*
Asymmetry	–	*
Broken blade tip	–	*
Worn blade	–	*
Worn hilt	–	**

Source: information from Wall (1987).

Notes
* Contrasts at the 90% significance level.
** Contrasts at the 99% significance level.

Table 3.2 The possible careers of Bronze Age metalwork, as evidenced by finds from the River Thames

Production	➤					*Deposition*
Production	➤	Destruction			➤	*Deposition* of damaged object
Production	➤	Use	➤	Recycling		
Production	➤	Use	➤	Recycling	➤	*Deposition* of residue
Production	➤	Use	➤			*Deposition* of intact object
Production	➤	Use	➤	Destruction	➤	*Deposition* of damaged object

Age – they could be employed in combat, as display items or as votive offerings. Weapons that had been used in fighting might either be deposited in the river without any further treatment, or they could first be damaged. Another option would be to recycle discarded objects and to use the raw material to make other artefacts, in which case a small fraction of the broken pieces might be committed to the ground. York's study shows how complicated these decisions might have been and how they seem to have varied from one period to another. At different times during the Later Bronze Age, between 75 and 86 per cent of the weapons had been used before they entered the water, but more of the spearheads were deliberately damaged in the Penard phase and more of the swords during the Wilburton and Ewart Park periods. While the ratio of used to unused weapons remained about the same, a growing proportion of this material was disabled. None of the Early Bronze Age artefacts had been treated in this way but it applied to about a fifth of the Middle Bronze Age items and to half of those dated to the Late Bronze Age. As this ritual increased in importance people inflicted more damage on the items they deposited in the river.

What applies to swords and spears applies to other kinds of metalwork as well. Vandkilde (1999) has studied the role of axes in Bronze Age Denmark. At the end of the Late Neolithic period and in Period 1A of the Early Bronze Age there seems to have been a continuum among the finds of axe heads. It extends from elaborately decorated examples to much simpler forms, but all of them provide similar evidence of use and resharpening. In Period 1B, however, the situation changes. Now there seem to have been two different kinds of axe heads. One was long, slender and carefully made. Some examples were decorated, and the axes of this kind were left unsharpened. The other form she describes as 'small, inconspicuous, coarse and often damaged' (ibid.: 260). The two forms have quite different associations. The work axes occur as single finds or in hoards which contain only one kind of artefact. The more elaborate examples are found together with other objects in what Vandkilde considers to be high status burials, but they also occur in hoards containing a wider variety of types. In this case the difference of style is clearly related to the ways in which these objects were used, but it may also relate to their individual life histories, for the striking contrasts in their condition and evidence for reworking suggest that they had circulated over different lengths of time.

In the same way, pots could have had a special significance in prehistory and for that reason their chronology may not be as straightforward as is sometimes supposed. Woodward (1999) has recently argued that ceramics did not play a central role in domestic life in Britain until the middle of the Iron Age. Individual vessels may have had a particular importance related to their contents, their decoration, the materials out of which they were made or the transactions in which they were used.

Several successive styles of pottery in prehistoric Britain illustrate this point. The first is Grooved Ware, a Late Neolithic ceramic tradition that seems to have originated in Orkney. Its special significance may be illustrated by the way in which certain vessels were decorated with similar motifs to those on the walls of houses and tombs. On the British mainland this style of pottery is associated with ceremonial sites and has often been found in structured deposits together with non-local artefacts. One reason for suggesting the significance of particular vessels is the care that was obviously taken to mend them when they broke. Grooved Ware pots were repaired approximately four times as often as other ceramics in this period, suggesting that the history of individual vessels was important (Cleal 1988). Moreover, some of those that were repaired were eventually incorporated in formal deposits at henges.

Three main types of vessels eventually took the place of Grooved Ware: first Beakers, and then Food Vessels and Collared Urns. None of them is easy to analyse according to an orthodox chronology. In each case that seems to be because of the overriding influence of the past. British Beakers show a rather similar range of styles to those in Northern Europe, but there the comparison breaks down. Although it is possible to devise a chronology for these different vessels, based on their form, their decoration and the artefacts associated with them, this scheme receives little support from radiocarbon dating (Kinnes *et al.* 1991). That is particularly surprising because in the Netherlands a similar sequence is confirmed by exactly the same method. How can we explain the discrepancy? The obvious objections seem to be unsatisfactory – the samples from Britain were carefully chosen and other dates from the same laboratory have conformed to expectations – so one response has been to question the Continental sequence itself. This seems ill advised. It might be wiser to investigate the assumptions that lie behind the British dating programme. Given the evidence that vessels in an earlier style had been mended to prolong their life span, it is illogical to employ samples associated with the final use of Beaker vessels to determine when those pots had been made. Individual examples may have circulated over a considerable period of time before they entered the archaeological record, and the radiocarbon dates refer to their deposition rather than their production. That may be why some of these dates were later than had been expected. It would also explain why worn or incomplete ceramic vessels were deposited in a number of graves during this period (Woodward 2000: 58–60). Again that might have happened because they had taken on a special significance.

Table 3.3 The conventional ceramic chronology for Southern Britain 3000–2000 BC
and the modifications suggested by studying the life histories of the successive
styles of pottery

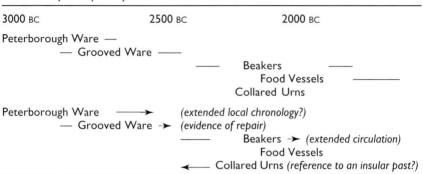

Beakers were succeeded by two other styles of pottery, although the chronologies of all three types overlapped. Food Vessels and Collared Urns both show
the influence of Beaker technology, but to varying extents these vessels also recall
the much older 'Peterborough' tradition, a style of highly decorated ceramics
which had been widely distributed before the adoption of Grooved Ware.
Indeed, the resemblance between these traditions was so strong that Longworth
(1984) developed a typology for Collared Urns based on their gradual diverg-
ence from that prototype. The usefulness of his scheme has been questioned
because of radiocarbon dates which suggest that Peterborough Ware was earlier
than he had supposed (Gibson and Kinnes 1997). That does not take into
account the possibility that Peterborough Ware lasted longer in some areas than
in others, yet there must be some explanation for its striking resemblance to Early
Bronze Age vessels.

Their wider associations suggests a solution to the problem. Whatever their
chronology, British and Irish Beakers were explicitly linked to an origin in Continental Europe. This was also the source of the earliest metalwork in these islands.
The origins of Food Vessels and Collared Urns remain in doubt, but these
traditions were an entirely insular development. Perhaps this is an illustration of
the 'rhetoric' of material culture, discussed in Chapter 1. Could it be that Food
Vessels and Collared Urns, with their apparent references back to an archaic
style of ceramics, were being used in reaction to the changes associated with the
use of Beakers? If so, then this development referred to the local rather than the
exotic. More than that, it was a reaction that could only be interpreted as an
explicit reference to the past (Table 3.3).

Moving house

The first of the case studies in Chapter 2 concerned the long houses of the
Linearbandkeramik. Although that discussion was mainly about origin myths, it

made the point that these particular buildings seem to have been vacated at regular intervals. They may well have been abandoned while they were structurally sound and seem to have been replaced in quite different positions within the settlement. There was a regular relationship between the abandoned long houses and their successors, for buildings in both groups followed the same alignment and were spaced at approximately equal intervals across the occupied area. Some of the older structures may have been replaced on the death of one of the occupants, and it seemed possible that the settlements of the Linear Pottery Culture were characterised by dwellings of the living interspersed with houses of the dead.

Although these Neolithic settlements have many features that are not found at other sites – the progressive lengthening of the buildings over time, the symbolic role of borrow pits, their association with child burials, and the distinctive orientations of the doorways – it is surprising how widely long houses are distributed in prehistoric Europe and how often these particular structures took on special connotations. Just as Neolithic houses can no longer be interpreted entirely in practical terms, the same applies to the later prehistoric buildings of Northern Europe.

One of the best known settlement sites in the Netherlands was also one of the first to be published in detail. This is the Middle and Late Bronze Age site at Elp, which was investigated by Waterbolk in the early 1960s (Waterbolk 1961 and 1964). Although many other settlements have been recorded since then, his changing interpretation of this particular site raises some points of relevance to the present argument. How did successive generations regard the dwellings of the immediate past? And how far were their own actions influenced by their awareness of history?

The settlement at Elp was discovered entirely by chance during the excavation of an adjacent burial mound and subsequent work identified the post holes of a considerable number of timber buildings. According to Waterbolk's estimate, there were six large houses, four smaller houses, three barns, five sheds and traces of at least another half dozen rectangular clusters of post holes. None of these overlapped with the position of the barrow, which had two central graves and further inhumations arranged in an arc around its perimeter. Nearby there was a smaller group of burials, laid out on the same alignment as the primary deposits in the neighbouring monument. The limits of two of the graves were marked by posts and all four burials may once have been covered by a mound.

The houses and other buildings in the settlement were laid out on two alignments, almost at right angles to one another (Figure 3.1). It was clear from the outset that the structures within the settlement had been built over a long period. Two pairs of buildings shared the same axis but their positions overlapped. There were also four cases in which individual houses cut across one another at approximately 90 degrees. Waterbolk's original interpretation of the site depended on three lines of argument. Occasionally it was possible to observe the stratigraphic relationship between overlapping buildings, and a few contexts on

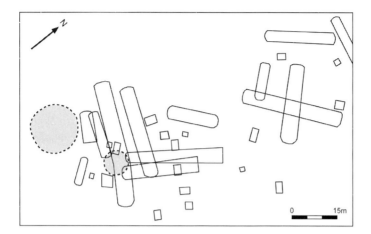

Figure 3.1 Excavated houses and barrows at Elp, Netherlands.

Source: information from Waterbolk (1961, 1964 and 1986).

the site produced radiocarbon dates. There were not many finds of artefacts from the excavation, but by combining these different sources of information he was able to suggest that a basic settlement module consisting of a major house, a subsidiary dwelling and one or more ancillary buildings had been replaced on at least five occasions. The burials at Elp belonged to the same period as the settlement.

More recent work has led him to revise his interpretation (Waterbolk 1986) (Figure 3.2a–c). Two developments have been particularly important here. First, calibration of the radiocarbon dates means that occupation must now be spread over about 800 years. Assuming that each long house could be used for about three decades – an estimate which has been made on other sites – that would mean that Elp could not have been occupied continuously. At the same time, settlement excavations in the Netherlands have led to the identification of a number of well dated building types, and these provide another basis for postulating the sequence at Elp.

A more recent interpretation by the excavator involves ten structural phases on the site. The settlement usually consisted of a major and a minor house and a set of ancillary buildings, some of which would now be considered as granaries. The small group of inhumations is thought to date from the same period as certain of these structures, although the palisaded round barrow could be older. In Waterbolk's new scheme the earliest house was built next to that barrow, but thereafter the main focus of the settled area shifted with each generation of buildings. The orientations of the houses changed four times during the period of occupation but normally the same axis was maintained across two or three successive phases before that happened. It is quite possible that these transitions occurred after intervals during which the site went out of use.

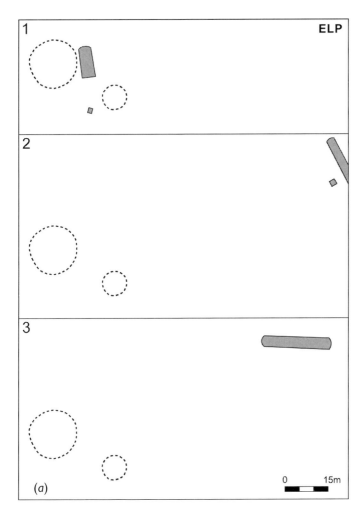

Figure 3.2a–c The structural sequence at Elp according to Waterbolk (1986).

Note
The positions of buildings are stippled and barrows are indicated by dashed lines.

Waterbolk is cautious in postulating this sequence but the details of his scheme are not important here. What is more significant are a number of features that receive little comment in his paper, for they suggest how the inhabitants of Elp responded to the past history of the site.

The alignment of the houses is remarkable (Figure 3.3). No matter how the structural sequence is organised, five of these buildings follow the same axis as the major graves: the two primary burials beneath the palisaded round barrow, and four more examples in a small cluster nearby – it may be no coincidence that

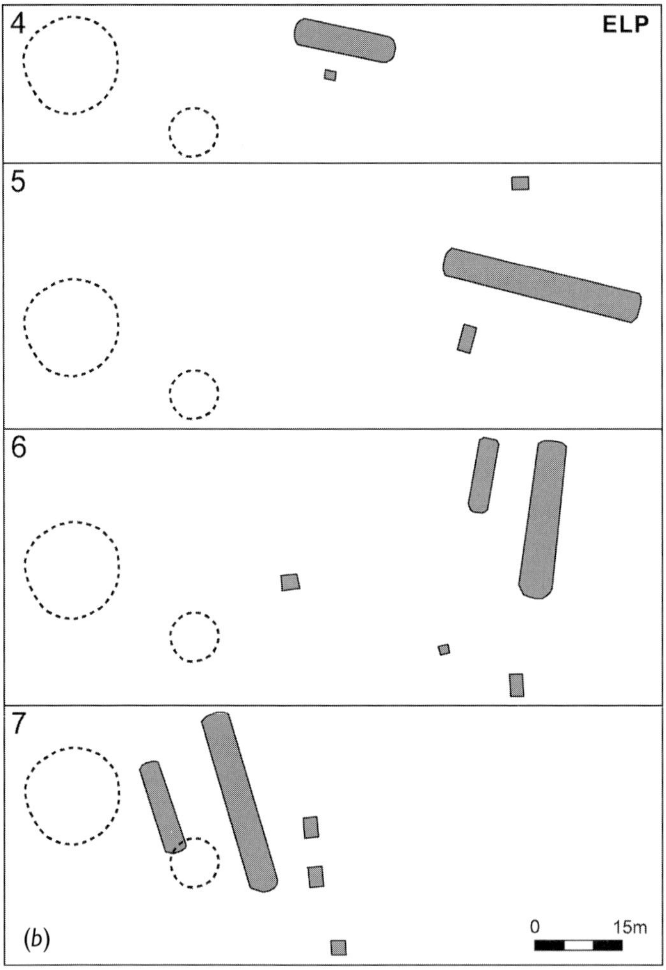

Figure 3.2b

so many of the buildings are immediately adjacent to this cemetery. The same axis is emphasised by the positions of the burials around the outer edge of the barrow, all but one of which are distributed between the north-east and south-west. That may also be relevant as five of the long houses at Elp adopt a rather similar axis.

Another five of the timber buildings were laid out almost at right angles to this alignment but their precise positions seem to have been chosen with some care. Although all of them are directed towards the larger barrow, *their orientations narrowly avoid it.* In two cases they pass its north-western flank and in two others they extend just outside its south-eastern limit. It seems as if the orientation of the graves influenced the positioning of the houses, yet the location of the mound

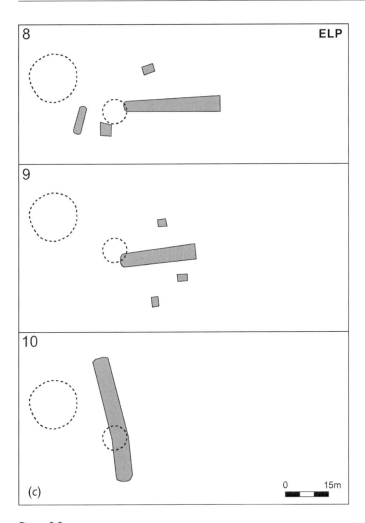

Figure 3.2c

that covered them was ignored. That is particularly interesting as none of those graves had been marked.

According to Waterbolk's revised chronology for Elp, the second group of burials is contemporary with the use of part of the settlement, and it is certainly true that from that stage onwards they seem to have provided an important focus of attention. No fewer than three of the houses are aligned on the position of this small cemetery and the buildings terminate at the limit of what may have been a covering mound. One of these buildings follows the same axis as the graves. The relationship between these structures and the cemetery can hardly be fortuitous because in each case the end wall of the house was no more than two metres away from the nearest burial. There is one exception to this trend. The longest of all the

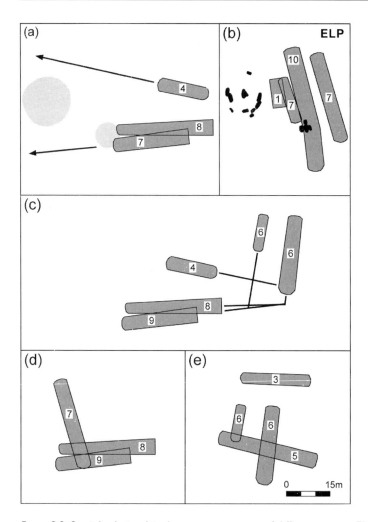

Figure 3.3 Spatial relationships between structures of different ages at Elp.

Notes
The numbers on each building are the phases to which they are assigned by Waterbolk (1986).
(a) Shows the alignment of the houses in relation to the positions of two barrows; (b) shows
their orientation in relation to that of the graves; (c) shows how buildings of different phases
seem to have been aligned on the same part of the site; (d) suggests that the positions of
successive houses may have referenced those of their predecessors; and (e) shows the same
process in relation to the ends and doorways of the buildings.

buildings at Elp actually cuts across the position of these four graves. Again that
relationship is unlikely to be accidental, for not only does this building follow
the same alignment as the burials, the side walls of the long house change
direction by two degrees where they cut across the cemetery. In Waterbolk's

interpretation, which is supported by pottery and radiocarbon dating, this was the last structure to be built before the site was abandoned.

If there is a complex relationship between the positions of the houses and those of the burials at Elp, the same applies to some of the successive buildings in the settlement. It is not just that these followed two basic alignments, for the plans of individual houses seem to have acknowledged those of their predecessors. That is the case even when the use of those buildings was separated by a significant length of time in Waterbolk's scheme. Thus different buildings adopted distinct alignments yet they ended at exactly the same position within the excavated area, as if each had been directed towards a common point. Alternatively, newer long houses may have extended just far enough to take in the site of an older building. Even then, the relationship may have been carefully contrived so that in one case a newly built house cut across the exact centre of one of its predecessors.

There appears to have been some order to this arrangement. Whether or not the excavator's sequence is right, it seems to have been important that houses built in different (but not necessarily successive) phases *should touch the positions of the older buildings. These could no longer have been standing when the newer houses were constructed.* Moreover, it was often enough to incorporate the point where an older building had ended or even to cut across the position of its doorway. Several of the principal buildings seem to have acknowledged the existence of earlier structures on the site just as their layout was also related to the positions and orientations of the burials towards the edge of the settlement. It goes without saying that such evidence is rather tenuous, but these relationships are repeated so often that they are likely to be significant. It seems possible that the positions of older houses were known even when their structures had vanished.

The process of house abandonment is as important here as it was in the Linearbandkeramik. Waterbolk excavated a number of pits at Elp and noted that they contained most of the artefacts on the site. He associated them directly with the occupation of the houses, and in many cases that could be true, but there are other instances in which the layout of the separate pits makes little sense in relation to the plans of these buildings (Figure 3.4). Some structures contain many more pits than others and in certain cases these features seem to extend underneath the side walls. In such instances the excavator has been forced to postulate the original positions of the posts that supported the roof. Surely a simpler explanation is that some of these pits were dug after the active use of these houses was over. They may have been opened when some of the raw material was retrieved or after these structures had been abandoned, but the fact that they cluster in the positions of certain of these buildings may provide another reason for supposing that those places still retained their significance. One wonders whether the artefacts found inside these pits had all accumulated by chance.

The excavation of Elp raises questions about the occupation of later pre-historic settlements in Northern Europe, but the evidence from this one site is not sufficient to answer them. More recent work in the same region has supplied some of the missing detail. In particular, Gerritsen (1999) has investigated the

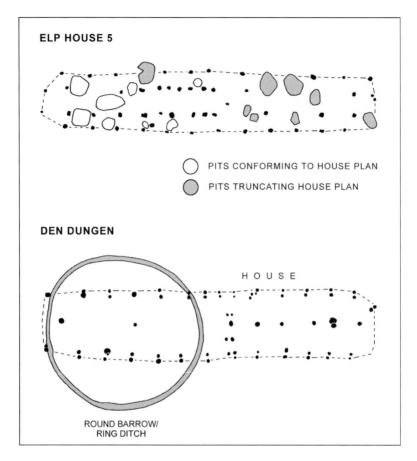

Figure 3.4 Bronze Age houses at Elp and Den Dungen, Netherlands, illustrating their relationships to pits and an earlier ring ditch.

Source: information from Waterbolk (1964) and Fokkens and Roymans (1991).

Notes
At Elp, one group of pits respects the positions of the structural supports while another ignores them and may have been dug after the house had gone out of use. At Den Dungen, one end of the house incorporates the site of an older barrow or ring ditch.

problems of house abandonment in the Late Bronze Age and Iron Age, and his work helps to account for some of the anomalies identified by Waterbolk's report.

Gerritsen's study begins with the Late Bronze Age, the period in which occupation at Elp came to an end, but it emphasises three of the features that are found on that site. First of all, the houses at Elp were not especially durable structures. With just two exceptions, there is little evidence that any of the posts had been renewed before the buildings were abandoned. Second, it is clear that these houses were nearly always replaced on different sites. Even when their positions overlapped, it was uncommon for successive buildings to be constructed in exactly the same positions. The third observation arises from the radiocarbon dates for Elp. However long individual houses were inhabited, it is quite clear that there were not sufficient buildings to allow occupation to have lasted for 800 years. The inhabitants must have moved to other locations for part of that time, even if the structures of the 'missing' periods were only a short distance outside the excavated area.

Gerritsen points out that these are the defining characteristics of what have become known as 'wandering' settlements: sites whose various components change their positions over quite short periods of time. They are found over a wide area extending from Belgium to Denmark and seem to have been occupied during the later part of the Bronze Age and the Early and Middle Iron Ages.

Interpretations of this evidence have changed over the years, but, in common with the settlements of the Linearbandkeramik, these sites are usually considered in strictly functional terms. It has been claimed that the life span of Bronze Age and earlier Iron Age houses in the Netherlands was determined by two main factors: the period over which these buildings would remain structurally sound, and the fertility of the surrounding farmland. The individual timbers in these houses might have lasted between 25 and 40 years according to local conditions, while it is often argued that settlements moved from one site to another because of the decreasing productivity of the soil. That only changed when the 'Celtic' field system was replaced by a new agricultural regime.

Neither proposition is entirely sound. Waterbolk's excavation at Elp found that only two of the houses – both of them among the smaller structures – showed much sign of rebuilding, although all the dwellings on the site ought to have been equally vulnerable to decay. The same applies to other well excavated settlements in the Netherlands and Belgium. For example, some of the houses at Colmschata, Donk and Den Dungen seem to have been repaired but others had not, while at Loon op Zand it seems as if different houses had been renovated to varying extents (Fokkens and Roymans 1991: 31–40, 111–27, 163–70 and 181–91). The relationship between settlements and the surrounding land raises just as many problems, and Gerritsen (1999) observes that there is little evidence of agricultural reorganisation.

Instead of emphasising purely ecological factors, he proposes a 'biographical' approach which considers the changing history of these houses in relation to the life cycle of the people who lived there. Drawing on ethnographic analogy, he suggests that the best way of accounting for these distinctive patterns is to suggest that the use of particular buildings was determined not by the structural life of the house but by the social life span of the household. Many of these buildings lasted a generation before they were replaced in a different position, and that might have happened because they were deserted on the death of one of the occupants. It could account for the apparent regularities observed in the construction and abandonment of these dwellings, but it could also explain why certain of the buildings had such a short period of use. Occupation might have ended because the head of a household had died prematurely. That would certainly explain the lack of repairs to some of these buildings and the different extents to which others seem to have been rebuilt.

Thus far Gerritsen's account resembles the interpretation of Linearband-keramik long houses put forward in Chapter 2. It is worth emphasising that both these case studies were arrived at quite independently, although they have certainly been influenced by the same ethnographic sources. In the Netherlands, there are other details which suggest that a purely functional model is inadequate. These include some of the features that have already been identified at Elp.

First, there is the orientation of later prehistoric houses. This has been studied by Therkorn (1987), who has noticed an interesting pattern. For the most part these buildings adopt two principal alignments: from north-east to south-west and from north-west to south-east. The second of these orientations is commonly found among the Celtic Fields of the same date. By contrast, she observes that ritual structures of that period adopt a different axis, so that human burials are generally directed towards the cardinal points. In this respect Elp is obviously anomalous, but on later sites this consideration becomes more important.

Second, there are a series of distinctive offerings associated with the first establishment of the houses. Again these suggest that such structures were incorporated into a wider conceptual scheme. Such deposits were not identified at Elp and may have been a more important element at later settlements, including those of the Roman Iron Age. At different sites they include the burial of an entire ox, substantial parts of the skeletons of horses, cows and dogs, a complete pot containing part of a cattle skull, cremated bone and smaller offerings of meat and grain (Therkorn 1987; Gerritsen 1999). These were generally associated with contexts that must date from the construction of the house, including deposits that had been buried beneath the roof supports, side walls and internal subdivisions; others were placed underneath the hearth. In some of the houses dating from the Later Iron Age and Roman periods hearths also contained large deposits of broken pottery laid out in a formal pattern and concealed by a covering of clay. Again these are likely to date from the earliest use of the building.

Lastly, it seems as if further deposits were provided when the houses were abandoned. This may account for the contents of some of the pits at Elp and could also explain the discovery of large groups of artefacts in the prehistoric wells at Oss (Fokkens 1998). Gerritsen draws attention to a number of distinctive deposits which seem to be connected with recently deserted houses. There are large deposits of pottery and other artefacts, but there are also features associated with evidence of fire, although there is nothing to suggest that most of the houses were burnt down. These 'closing deposits' include unusually rich collections of cultural material and quantities of grain. In two cases the abandoned houses contained complete ceramic vessels. As we have seen, large amounts of pottery had also been concealed in the base of the hearth as the building was constructed. It is surely significant that those hearths were left intact when occupation ceased.

In some cases it seems as if material was retrieved from abandoned buildings and incorporated in the structure of the houses that took their place, but the extent of this practice is uncertain. Gerritsen suggests that a number of the houses were allowed to decay *in situ*, in the way that seems to have happened during the Linearbandkeramik. On the other hand, the work of the Assendelver Polders Project suggested that in the later settlements building material was recycled, even when the houses were replaced at different locations (Therkorn and Abbink 1987). That evidence is particularly convincing as the remains of these buildings had been preserved by waterlogging. In such cases the continuity of the household from one generation to another could have been expressed by incorporating parts of each successive building in the structure that replaced it.

There is another reason for emphasising the importance of the past in the creation and operation of such sites, and again it is provided by the Assendelver Polders Project. This took place in a region in which settlement sites had been preserved by the high water table. Some of them occupied low mounds which raised them above the level of the surrounding area. They are the equivalent of the settlement mounds or *terpen* found in other parts of the Netherlands. It has always been supposed that the development of these earthworks was to be explained in functional terms, for they were associated with a livestock economy and would have kept animals dry during periods of flooding. In the Assendelver Polders Project this interpretation has been challenged by Therkorn and Abbink, who observe that such mounds normally developed during the later phases of occupation on any particular site (Table 3.4). They argue that these earthworks would have been unnecessary because there was sufficient natural drainage at the time:

> We suggest that raising certain areas on the levees did not take place as a 'response' to environmental changes relating to a rising ground-water table; rather, the new practice of building platforms was mainly determined by . . . socio-economic factors.
>
> (1987: 142)

What were these factors? Some of the platforms were built over the sites of earlier

Table 3.4 The main structural sequences at excavated sites in the Assendelver Polders

			Number of separate sequences
Small fields	to	house or post structure	5
Small fields	to	small platform	5
Houses or post structures	to	house on platform	3
Houses or post structures	to	empty platform	7
Small platform	to	large platform	3

Source: information from Therkorn and Abbink (1987).

houses and would have marked their positions for later generations. In fact they might have commemorated the people who had lived there. That is not to suggest that the platforms were mortuary monuments, but, like the barrows of earlier periods, they would have helped to recall the importance of the dead in the daily lives of their descendants.

That last example extends into the Roman Iron Age when the currency of wandering settlements had come at an end, but it adds weight to some of the observations that have been made at older settlement sites. It seems as if the use of the separate dwellings went through a cycle that mirrored the lives of the occupants, so that domestic structures needed to be replaced when the head of a household died. The hearth was among the first features to be constructed when a new house was built and it had a specialised deposit of pottery concealed underneath it. That hearth remained a major focus of activity within the building, and it was carefully preserved when the house was abandoned. The erection of some of these structures may have entailed the provision of offerings at key positions in the dwelling, just as others may have been required when occupation came to an end.

The orientations of the houses might be used to form other connections between the past and the present. Individual houses could be aligned on one another or even on the positions where structures had stood in the past, and there are settlement sites in which whole groups of buildings shared the same orientation as one another. These alignments may have changed at intervals in the life of the site, but in general terms the houses followed similar axes to the Celtic Fields of the Iron Age and avoided the less propitious orientations connected with the dead. There may be a way of explaining these relationships, for the fields and the houses would have shared an emphasis on the position of the sun at the solstices. The choice of these orientations linked the fortunes of the living to the timeless cycle of the seasons. Perhaps the dead no longer played a part in everyday affairs and so their graves could adopt a different alignment. At the same time, people obviously paid them a continuing respect. Thus the houses at Elp are directed towards two small barrows, and at Den Dungen a similar building is aligned on an earlier ring ditch and extends into its interior (Fokkens and Roymans 1991: 163–70) (see Figure 3.4). The same relationship is apparent in the Roman Iron Age settlement of Oss where another rectangular house links the positions of two Late Iron Age ring ditches and overlaps with both these monuments (Wesselinger 2000).

If there is one site that illustrates the full complexity of these relationships it is Hijken in the Northern Netherlands (Harsema 1992) (Figures 3.5 and 3.6). Here a group of Middle Bronze Age houses was identified by excavation. They were set within a curvilinear enclosure which is interpreted as a cattle compound and were orientated from south-east to north-west. Just over 300 metres away was a barrow cemetery of the same date, but the long axes of these houses was directed away from the mounds (although their doorways could have faced in that direction). During the Iron Age, a field system was created around these barrows

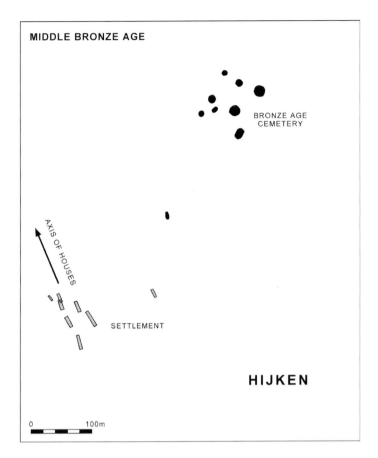

Figure 3.5 The organisation of the Bronze Age landscape at Hijken, Netherlands.
Source: information from Harsema (1992).

and extended across the site of the Bronze Age settlement, following the alignment of the older houses. These fields seem to have been associated with a second
group of domestic buildings which was laid out parallel to the newly established
land boundaries. Some of them overlapped the positions of the earlier buildings
but they adopted a quite different axis, with the result that now they were
orientated on the Bronze Age cemetery where new burial mounds were built.
There is a fascinating interplay between the different elements in this sequence.
The Middle Bronze Age houses remained quite separate from the barrows. The
later field system seems to have respected the alignment set up by the first generation of buildings, and yet the structures that were set within it were orientated
on the burial area. Every element in that landscape was influenced by the
relationship between the present and the past.

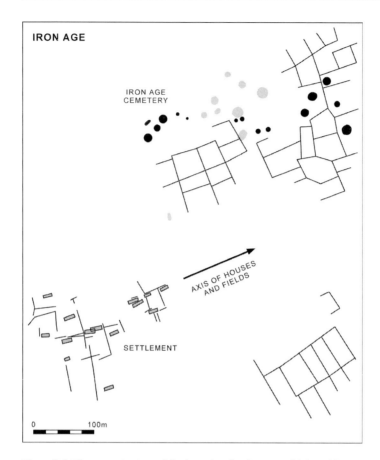

Figure 3.6 The organisation of the Iron Age landscape at Hijken, Netherlands.

Source: information from Harsema (1992).

Changing the landscape of Dartmoor

My previous study extended from the individual house to the local landscape, but it was a landscape with a small number of well defined elements: houses, burial mounds and fields. I shall end this chapter with an account of a more complicated sequence of development.

A suitable area for such an approach is Dartmoor, in South-West England. This is an upland region of what is now marginal land, although natural conditions seem to have been more favourable before the environment changed during the first millennium BC (Fleming 1988). Originally it seems to have offered a wide enough range of natural resources for large numbers of people to live there for at least part of the year. The fact that it was little used in subsequent periods means that a series of prehistoric sites survived largely undamaged until the moor was reused during the Middle Ages. Even today, it contains some of the best preserved prehistoric landscapes in Europe.

In recent years, Fleming (1988) has investigated the remarkable system of land divisions that have become known as the Dartmoor reaves. These are among the most extensive boundary systems recorded in Britain and they are also among the oldest. Large areas of the interior of the moor were delimited by low banks or walls, while similar structures were used to define a series of territories, each of them based on one of the river valleys radiating from the high ground. Within these land units there were large areas of fields, many of them organised around a series of parallel earthworks; for that reason Fleming describes them as 'co-axial' systems (Figure 3.7). Excavation has established that some of the banks

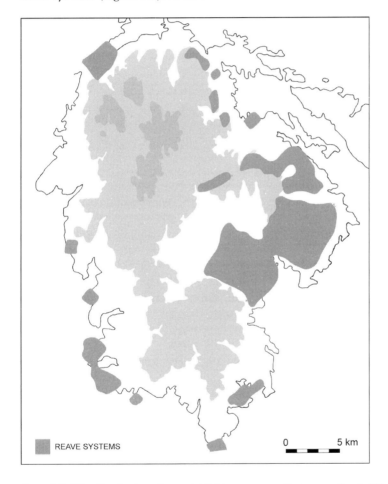

REAVE SYSTEMS

0   5 km

Figure 3.7 The distribution of co-axial field systems on Dartmoor, South-West England.

Source: information from Fleming (1988).

and walls replaced the lines of earlier fences, just as the stone-built round houses which are such a feature of Dartmoor's archaeology may be the successors of timber buildings. The account that follows draws on the work of Fleming (1988) and Butler (1991a, 1991b, 1993, 1994 and 1997).

One of the main lessons of Fleming's fieldwork has been the sheer scale on which land holding was organised and the amount of planning which must have gone into the creation of this system. These are important issues and that is why they have set the agenda for so much recent research. But the organised landscapes epitomised by the Dartmoor reaves were not established in a newly settled area: they came into being in a region that already bore the imprint of many generations of activity. Having discussed how individual settlements might have been influenced by memories of the past, we must consider how an entire landscape could be transformed. That is not so easy as earlier prehistoric activity on Dartmoor has rarely been investigated with that question in mind.

Its components are easy to identify, because some of them are associated with datable artefacts or are kinds of monument that have been studied in other parts of the country. Environmental evidence suggests that Dartmoor was used on an increasing scale from the mid third millennium BC, and this is consistent with the dating evidence provided by burials from the area (Fleming 1988: chapter 7). At first it may have been visited seasonally by communities from the surrounding lowlands, and it was not until about 1700 BC that the land was sub-divided by the reaves. In between, the archaeological record is dominated by specialised forms of monument: burial cairns, cists, stone rows and stone circles. Many of the houses visible on the moor could have begun life over the same period, but this has yet to be demonstrated by excavation.

There is some evidence of how these sites were organised in relation to one another. The cairns can be divided into two groups according to their size (Grinsell 1978) (Figure 3.8). Together with many of the cists, the smaller examples tend to be found close to major watercourses on the flanks of the valleys that lead down from the central plateau. This is where some of the stone round houses occur, and certain of them may well be contemporary with these monuments; at all events they occupy the parts of Dartmoor which were best suited to sustained occupation. The larger cairns – those over 20 metres in diameter – have a quite different distribution. They select prominent positions on the highest ground and can be seen over considerable distances. Their construction obviously involved more work than the remaining sites. All too little is known about the associated burials and it would be wrong to over-emphasise the importance of these cairns for, with one exception, the most complex grave goods of the Early Bronze Age are beyond the limits of the moor (Todd 1987: 138–50).

The other monuments are equally difficult to study but again their distributions are sharply characterised. There are not many stone circles on Dartmoor, but, like the burial cairns, these sites can be divided into two groups. The less regular examples occur on the lower part of the moor in the same areas as the living sites, while a second group of more precisely laid out circles is located on

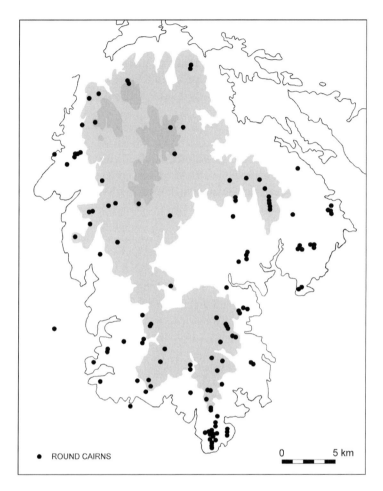

Figure 3.8 The distribution of large round cairns on Dartmoor, South-West England.
Source: information from Grinsell (1978).

the high ground beyond the distribution of most of the other monuments. These are sometimes difficult to find and cannot be seen from far away.

The stone rows appear to have played a major role in integrating these separate components. They take the form of single, double or multiple alignments and for the most part they extend uphill towards the positions of cairns and stone circles. Dartmoor stone rows vary considerably in scale, but often the monoliths were taller as they approached these sites.

Barnatt has suggested that these separate observations can be combined (1998: 98–102). Perhaps the higher ground of the moor was associated mainly with the dead and the supernatural, and it was here that the principal monuments were built. By contrast, the more hospitable areas on the lower ground provide the strongest evidence of settlement, and that is where smaller cairns and cists occur together with round houses. This may have been thought of as the domain of the living, in which case the creation of the stone rows would have formed a connection between those two worlds. They marked the paths along which the living and the dead could approach the sacred sites of the Early Bronze Age (Figure 3.9).

How did the past impinge on the landscape of the reaves? Two kinds of site had gone through distinctive life histories of their own. The stone rows may have been lengthened over time and certain examples were reinforced by other alignments of monoliths running parallel to them. When their construction was complete it seems as if they were blocked at their lower end. Some of the poorly dated houses may have followed a rather similar cycle. Not only were timber buildings eventually replaced in stone, certain of these houses seem to have become funerary monuments once their original use was over. There are a few examples in which part of the interior was converted into a cairn and other cases in which cists were constructed in their ruins (Butler 1997: 137). It even seems as if the entrances to some of these buildings had been blocked. On Shaugh Moor, for example, a ditch was excavated which cut off direct access to two of the houses (Wainwright and Smith 1980: figure 10).

These may be exceptional cases but there are other reasons for suggesting a direct link between the houses and the cairns. In common with those in other areas, the great majority of the round houses on Dartmoor have their doorways towards the south-east. This is also the alignment of the burial cists (Table 3.5), and the same relationship is suggested by the small number of stone circles in the area. In four cases the tallest monolith is towards the south-east or south-south-east, and on two other sites there is an outlier to the south-east or south. It

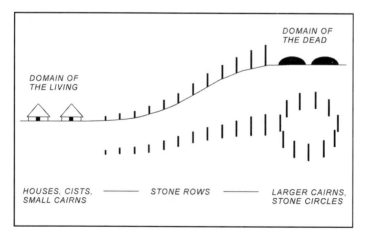

Figure 3.9 An interpretation of the role of stone rows in the Bronze Age landscape of Dartmoor, South-West England.

Table 3.5 The orientations of prehistoric sites on Dartmoor. As there are no entrances to the cists, each could have been directed in one of two possible directions

	North to east	East to south	South to west	West to north
Round houses (%)	4	62	32	2

	North to east/south to west		East to south/west to north	
Cists (%)	7		93	

Source: information from Butler (1997).

appears that some of the major monuments conformed to the same conceptual scheme. That is not true of the stone rows which seem to have been more closely related to the local topography and to the paths along which people approached the upland cairns. The same applies to the setting of the later reaves that followed the limits of the upland plateau and bounded the separate land blocks in the valleys. Again their course was closely related to the local topography.

One might expect the field systems to be equally sensitive to the terrain, but this is not always so. In some cases their parallel alignments cut across the grain of the country, in one case even extending across a gorge. That is not to say that they adopt a single alignment in the same way as the cists: rather, they follow a number of dominant axes in different parts of the moor, but they nearly always avoid the cardinal points. It would be wrong to exaggerate the accuracy with which this was achieved, but of the seventeen major systems distinguished by Fleming none extends north–south and just one is aligned east–west, even though individual groups of fields may drift off the preferred alignment. Nine adopt rather similar axes to the houses and cists and another seven are laid at right angles to that orientation. It may be no coincidence that is also the second commonest axis observed by the house doorways. Again it is necessary to emphasis that these patterns are not created entirely by the prevailing topo-graphy. It would be unusual for houses to have their doors on the uphill side because they might fill with water, but the main requirement would be for the field systems to face into the sun and this could just as well be achieved by directing them towards the south.

These are very general patterns but more local relationships can be identified, too. The major reaves extend over considerable distances but in doing so they often connect the positions of existing burial cairns. That relationship is usually interpreted in terms of practicalities, for these would have been prominent landmarks when the boundaries were built. By incorporating them into the new system they would be preserved.

It may be that they had a more basic significance for the communities who laid out the reaves. It would be perfectly possible to align these boundaries using natural features of the topography, such as the granite tors that occur so widely on Dartmoor, and in some cases that certainly happened. In others, the layout could have been organised by erecting stone or wooden markers or by lighting fires. During the Early Bronze Age the siting of the more prominent cairns showed a certain order and it seems just as likely that elements of that scheme were maintained and even emphasised by the building of the reaves (Figure 3.10). That would be consistent with the evidence from other prehistoric land-scapes in Britain, where barrows and cairns seem to have been employed in very much the same way. Indeed, there are sites where the boundary earthworks diverge from the most obvious path to take in a burial monument whose position can not be identified from any distance away (Bradley, Entwistle and Raymond 1994: chapters 7 and 8). In such cases it seems to have been important to involve particular monuments from the past in the creation of the new system.

The same relationship extends to the layout of the fields. In some cases the cairns were excluded from the enclosed area, as if to preserve their integrity, but in others they were built into the edges and corners of these plots. There is not much evidence to suggest that individual structures were destroyed or robbed of stone during this period, and when this happened it did not apply consistently from one class of monument to another. Thus cairns were occasionally damaged but stone circles were usually respected. We could almost say that the co-axial field systems of Dartmoor were a compromise between three competing factors: the need to settle the most suitable farmland; the necessity to organise the landscape according to the basic axes laid down by tradition; and an attempt to thread these fields around the cairns that already existed in the area.

Something similar applies to the Dartmoor stone rows. These exhibit a series of subtle relationship to the reaves. Like the rings of monoliths, they were usually treated with circumspection (see Figure 3.10). A number of the land boundaries established around the upper edge of the moorland run parallel to existing stone rows, leaving the older monuments intact by excluding them from the enclosed area. Sometimes the distance between these successive structures was as little as 5 metres, and yet the monoliths of the stone rows do not seem to have been taken

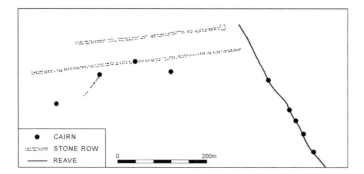

Figure 3.10 The relationship between stone rows, cairns and land boundaries at Merrivale, Dartmoor, South-West England.

Source: information from Butler (1997).

for building these boundaries. In other instances standing stones belonging to these alignments were preserved by incorporating them into the later construction. There are sites at which the reaves trace a careful path between a number of separate stone rows, as if to reduce any damage to their fabric, while in those cases in which they do cut across the older monuments there seems to have been an intention to disturb them as little as possible. Thus the locations of certain of the stone rows along the edges of the Dartmoor plateau seem to have influenced the layout of the land divisions that were built during a subsequent phase. There are cases in which the reaves either avoid the positions of these rows or adopt the same alignment themselves. In most instances there is evidence of a subtle accommodation with the past.

I mentioned that individual houses might have a complex history and that some of them could have been formally closed or converted into funerary monuments. In other cases they seem to have been treated rather like the cairns and stone rows, for their sites were preserved in the structures that took their place. It is difficult to discuss this observation. There are certain problems to consider – some of these buildings may have replaced wooden dwellings which can only be found by excavation; their relationships to enclosures and field walls are not obvious from surface inspection – yet the cumulative picture is both intriguing and convincing. Individual houses were incorporated into some of the longer reaves, they were frequently found in the corners and edges of fields, and they also played a pivotal role in the layout of domestic enclosures (Figure 3.11).

In many cases it is impossible to work out the sequence of construction without recourse to excavation, yet there are examples where the houses must surely have been the earliest structures on the site. Individual boundaries run up to houses in much the same way as they take in the positions of cairns. That is clear where the reaves are butted on to these buildings, and a similar relationship may explain how some of the groups of walled enclosures developed. In this case it seems as though successive enclosures abutted one another, so that it is possible to work out the evolution of a particular complex. That has been recognised for some time, but less attention has been paid to the way in which many of the junctions between successive walls were located at the precise positions of stone houses. In certain cases it is clear that this process would have made those buildings virtually inaccessible. There may be no sign of a doorway and it would have been difficult to reach these houses or to move between them and other parts of the site. The most likely explanation is that the ruins of older structures were used in planning later settlements (see Figure 3.11). That idea needs to be investigated by careful fieldwork, but it has an important corollary. If the sites of abandoned buildings were incorporated into the boundaries of settlements, why were their remains left intact? After all, they would have provided an ideal source of raw material, yet the very fact that the same relationships can be observed on so many different sites suggests that it did not happen. Like the stone rows and many of the cairns, these places were commemorated and respected. That is why the positions of those buildings can be identified today.

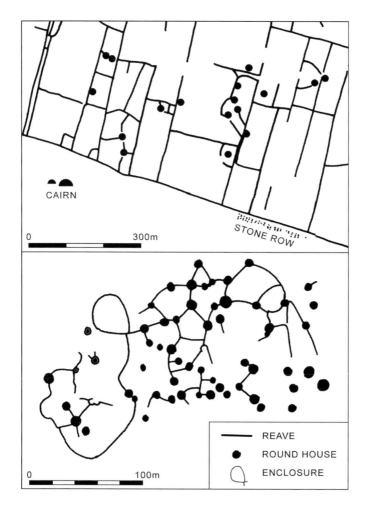

Figure 3.11　The relationship between houses, field boundaries and enclosure walls on
Dartmoor, South-West England. The upper map shows part of Holne Moor
and the lower map a series of conjoined enclosures on Standon Down.

Source: information from Fleming (1988) and Butler (1997).

A summary

Now it will be evident why I chose to compare the history of Bronze Age
settlements in the Netherlands and South-West England. There are superficial
similarities between these two areas – the close relationship between burial
monuments and living sites; the alignments of houses and field systems – but the
basic point is that in both cases the lives of any one generation were profoundly
affected by the visible traces of their predecessors. That is true of specialised

monuments like round barrows, stone circles and stone rows, but it is also true of domestic buildings. However different the ways in which these landscapes were inhabited, each of them would only have been comprehensible in terms of a sequence that grew out of the ruins of the past.

What applied to settlements and field systems applies to artefacts as well, for each of these had its own history. It took the form of a narrative that told where those objects had been made, how they had been used and the circumstances in which they changed hands. Some of those events would also have been apparent from the traces that they left behind on the artefacts themselves. Again the material culture of any one moment was implicated in the material culture of the past. People, houses, landscapes and portable objects all lived parallel lives and each of them would have provided a medium for human memory. Oral traditions were vitally important, but it was through an interplay between those accounts and the biographies of things that people without written documents were able to trace their histories.

Their projects extended into the future as well as the past. In the final section I have discussed the various ways in which specialised monuments were treated long after they had been built. There is a paradox here, for they may originally have been created to be remembered by posterity. That was not always to be. Their history poses so many problems that it provides the subject matter of the next chapter.

Chapter 4

Projecting future pasts

Monuments and the formation of memory

Reading *The Great Wall of China*

Monuments lead double lives. They are built in the present but often they are directed towards the future. For later generations, they come to represent the past. The word 'monument' derives from the Latin verb monere, to remind, and it is appropriate since some of them last for a very long time. Others may be levelled as soon as they are built.

Perhaps that is why monument building attracted the attention of one of the masters of paradox. In 1917, the Czech writer Franz Kafka composed his short story, *The Great Wall of China*. The text was never finished and the surviving fragment was first published some years after his death (Kafka 1963a [1931]). It shows how difficult it is to come to terms with this phenomenon.

The story reflects on the building of the wall, on the character of its original design and also on the ways in which different people understood the project. It starts with a striking observation. Although the wall was intended to protect China from her enemies in the north, it had been constructed in sections. These were separated by wide intervals of open ground, some of which were closed after the announcement that the entire edifice had been finished. Indeed, the narrator suspects that some of the gaps were never filled at all.

How could the wall have protected anyone when it was not built as a continuous structure? Kafka supplies an unexpected answer. People 'were trying to join forces . . . for the achievement of a single aim' (1963a: 239), yet the scale of the task was so great that the workers had to be brought from every part of the country. Each segment was as much as any one group could complete within a reasonable period. It took 5 years to build 500 metres of wall; but by that time the supervisors were demoralised. It was only when they had left their completed sections and saw other lengths that they regained their confidence in the project. Now they realised that they were engaged in a common task, so that *the construction of the monument would also have helped to build the fabric of society*. The teams came to understand that they formed parts of a larger whole, just like the segments of the wall.

But, for the storyteller, the function of the wall is difficult to explain even in these terms. He has never encountered the hostile peoples of the north and knows them only from the pictures he shows his children. The country extends so far that no invading force can overcome it:

> We have not seen them and if we remain in our villages we shall never see them, even if on their wild horses they should ride as hard as they can straight towards us – the land is too vast and would not let them reach us, they would end their course in the empty air . . .
>
> (Kafka 1963a: 241)

In that case why did so many people leave their homes to make their contribution to this project? According to the narrator, that is 'a question for the high command' (ibid.: 239).

Yet no one knows the nature of the high command. It is a mysterious institution whose history may go back to the creation. The source of its authority is equally obscure, but its activities apparently enjoy the approval of the gods. The plans for the construction of the wall have always existed, for they were conceived at the beginning of time. But if that is true, then the threat from the north is simply a pretext and the entire project is absurd:

> I believe that the high command has existed from all eternity, and the decision to build the wall likewise. Unwitting peoples of the north, who imagined they were the cause of it! Honest, unwitting Emperor, who imagined that he decreed it! We builders of the wall know that it was not so and hold our tongues.
>
> (ibid.: 242)

The conclusion is inescapable: the very people who constructed the Great Wall of China did not know why it was built. Was it to be explained in simple functional terms, or was it really a project directed towards the supernatural: an enterprise that had the endorsement of the gods? No one could be certain.

Kafka begins his story by questioning the practical effectiveness of the wall. He considers its political role as a way of mobilising society, but now he is forced to conclude that *the project exists for its own sake*. It has another aspect, too. His narrator compares its construction with the building of the Tower of Babel in the *Book of Genesis*. He tells us of a plan to use the firm foundation of the wall to build a still greater tower to overshadow that famous project. So the Great Wall of China is not a defensive work at all but an attempt to emulate the achievements of the past. The tower would be directed towards the heavens and the finished structure would assume a metaphysical significance very different from its original role as military architecture. In that guise it would have retained its significance for ever.

If the construction of certain monuments involves an attempt to influence people in the future, that is rarely achieved. Meanings change, and the interpretation of monuments often escapes the intentions of those who build them. In fact there is an analogy between the construction of the wall, which may never have been completed, and the history of Kafka's own manuscript. *The Great Wall of China* is a fragment, which is sometimes published together with another incomplete piece, *The News of the Building of the Wall* (Kafka 1963b). It is not clear whether they both formed parts of the same project or how either of these texts was intended to develop. Kafka does not seem to have communicated his plans for completing the narrative and, as a result, what remains can be interpreted in different ways. On one level it is a parable about the exercise of power, but, as we shall see, it says just as much about the limits of human knowledge and the uncertainties brought about by the passage of time. Indeed, it may be that its meanings have changed entirely in the light of the political history of Central Europe since Kafka's death in 1924. No author has unlimited control over the ways in which his or her work will be interpreted, and that is especially true of unfinished texts.

This comparison between monument building and writing is hardly new. Many people have compared material culture with texts and Thomas has even discussed the different ways of 'reading' monuments' (1999: chapter 3). Like the writings of Kafka, they are intended to convey a message to other people, extending beyond the lives of the original authors. At the same time, those intentions will be interpreted – and perhaps misunderstood – by later generations. That is because they will approach these statements according to their own experience and preoccupations. Monuments may have been created to remind future generations of the beliefs and achievements of the past, but it is impossible to exercise so much influence over the memories of one's successors.

This is made clear in the second part of the story.

The Chinese people are particularly loyal to their Emperor, and that is how they are persuaded to build the wall in the first place. But the sheer size of the country creates problems. Just as the narrator has never seen the enemy forces whom the wall is meant to exclude, he has never encountered the Emperor and has had little or no contact with his officials. News travels slowly across such enormous spaces, and when it arrives it is out of date. Whole communities do their best to obey the orders of a ruler that may have taken many years to reach them.

That would even apply to the reasons for constructing the wall. The information would have been transformed as it passed from one area to another. However determined the high command might be to convey a unified message to the world, it would never succeed. Still less could such a consistent vision be imposed on later generations. The passage of information across China is very similar to its transmission over time. No one is quite sure which Emperor is reigning or even which dynasty is in power. People obey orders that were issued in the distant past, 'but the living ruler they confuse among the dead' (Kafka 1963a: 245). Whatever can be discovered must be interpreted in terms of local knowledge. Kafka sums up the situation in a characteristic paradox:

If from such appearances anyone should draw the conclusion that in reality we have no Emperor, he would not be far from the truth. Over and over again it must be repeated. There is perhaps no people more faithful to the Emperor than ours in the south, but the Emperor derives no advantage from our fidelity. . . . The result of holding such opinions is a life on the whole free and unconstrained. . . . a life that is subject to no contemporary law, and attends only to exhortations and warnings that come to us from olden times.

(ibid.: 246)

The memories of the future

Kafka's parable was not written for prehistorians but it does echo a number of their concerns. It is never easy to explain why monuments were built, and the reasons may have varied from one section of society to another. Those monuments may appear to serve a practical function, and yet their scale is often out of all proportion to the ostensible reasons for building them. They may be constructed to enshrine a particular view of the world and to represent it in durable form to later generations (Renfrew 1998), yet once again that process is unlikely to succeed. Those structures will be interpreted and reinterpreted like Kafka's text, and they may provide just as much scope for individual creativity. Information cannot be transmitted completely accurately across the generations, and this results in the curious situation that monuments may be built to maintain the integrity of certain beliefs, yet the more durable the media that carry them the more likely it is that the projected audience will have opinions of its own. Certain monuments may have been designed to preserve a particular view of the past and to carry it forward into the future, but the history of these constructions shows how rarely this was achieved.

In fact there is no reason to suppose that all the constructions that have been described as monuments were built for exactly the same reasons. There is a certain circularity in this approach. Because individual monuments had a long history, it is commonly supposed that this was why they were built. In fact the sequences observed at different sites may have to be interpreted in a number of ways. Of course there are monuments where the original conception seems to have been respected and where the structural sequence amounts to little more than the repair and maintenance needed to ensure that they remained in use. That applies to some megalithic tombs. On the other hand, sites could have been utilised for similar lengths of time because the forms of individual monuments were modified in accordance with changing interpretations. In some cases their entire character might be altered and new kinds of construction might take the place of older ones. In still other instances novel types of building might be raised in the vicinity of existing monuments, so that the original scheme was compromised. It is not enough to know that particular sites were used over significant periods of time: it is also important to discover whether a single vision was respected throughout the archaeological sequence or whether it was modified or rejected during subsequent phases.

Nor should it be supposed that the history of all monuments was open-ended. It is difficult to think of any prehistoric site that remained in use indefinitely. Eventually, every one went out of commission, although the processes by which its history was brought to an end are as varied as the structural sequences themselves. Some typical examples are considered here.

Certain monuments have unusually short histories. This can happen in two ways. The first is where a monument may be built and immediately destroyed. This is really an instance of the wider process of 'remembering by forgetting' considered in Chapter 2, where it was illustrated by the distinctive treatment of statue menhirs. I shall consider other examples, but it is worth emphasising that in many instances this process was repeated at regular intervals, so that the removal of a particular monument might be followed soon afterwards by the creation of another structure of the same type. A good example might be the levelling and re-excavation of the ditches surrounding Neolithic enclosures (see p. 87).

In the second case the development of individual monuments may have followed a prescribed path extending over a fixed period of time from the first creation of that structure to its completion and abandonment. What the excavator might think of as the *structural sequence* could actually have been laid down from the outset, so that the successive modifications to the monument formed part of the rituals which were conducted there.

The remaining sections of this chapter explore the implications of different kinds of sequence. They begin with an account of the ritual cycle at a series of Neolithic and Early Bronze Age monuments in Scotland where these problems have been investigated by recent fieldwork. In these cases the sequence seems to have developed towards a predetermined conclusion. This case study involves a series of cairns and stone circles.

The discussion then considers a complex of timber and stone settings at Aosta in Northern Italy and investigates their changing relationship with a group of megalithic monuments. It examines the ways in which different structures were built, modified and replaced within a single site. Among these were statue menhirs, so I shall take up some of the points introduced in my account of Petit Chasseur.

The chapter ends with a third study which is more closely related to the issues raised by Kafka's story. This example concerns the bewildering variety of monuments found around Carnac in North-West France. It traces the outlines of still another kind of sequence, in which quite new kinds of construction may have been built in reaction to the earlier history of this region. This discussion is related to the account of Breton megaliths in Chapter 2, but in this case it covers a longer period of time.

In Scottish circles

Two recent papers have drawn attention to the unusual character of the sequence at particular monuments. The first is Thomas's discussion of the treatment of cursuses in Scotland (Thomas 2000).

A cursus is a long rectangular enclosure of a type that dates from the Neolithic period (Barclay and Harding 1999). Its distribution seems to be peculiar to Britain and Ireland, and the sites may be defined in several different ways. They can consist of a single ditch or bank enclosing an empty area. Other monuments incorporate a central mound, probably related to the long barrow, while in Scotland some cursuses seem to be delimited by a series of posts. These may be found inside earthwork enclosures or they can form entirely free-standing structures.

Those investigated by Thomas are in South-West Scotland where in one case an elongated post setting was found within an earthwork perimeter. A nearby example was completely free-standing. They are so distinctive because it seems as if the individual posts were burnt or uprooted from the ground before some of them were replaced in the same positions. In fact, the situation may be still more complicated as certain uprights survived from each monument to be incorporated in its successors while others were destroyed. A very similar pattern has been identified at Bannockburn closer to the east coast (Rideout 1997) (Figure 4.1).

Such cycles of destruction and replacement are not peculiar to those monuments. They can also be found at causewayed enclosures, whose chronology overlaps with that of these earthworks. In this case the spaces used for a variety of public events were defined by an interrupted ditch or ditches (the background to their building was discussed in Chapter 2). It is not clear whether all the ditch segments were dug simultaneously, but on most well excavated sites it is clear that the earthworks were periodically levelled: a process which resulted in the preservation of a series of placed deposits including human bones, animal remains, decorated pottery and a variety of artefacts. After a brief interval, the ditches were recut and the original form of the monument was re-established, but the work was usually undertaken with so much care that the existing offerings were not disturbed (Pryor 1998). The same practices continued at a number of smaller ring ditches, defined by pits or segmented earthworks, and they even extend to individual posts in the timber circle known as the Sanctuary (Pitts 2001).

Thomas compares these patterns with the conventional understanding of monuments:

> Durable monuments, principally those composed of earth and stone, had a mnemonic capacity. Their continued presence and re-use brought the past into the present. . . . But, alternatively, events which involved destruction and consumption, but which left no visible trace might be a means of inserting a place into tradition, making it worthy of remembering. . . . [This] recollection took on a physical aspect: re-using [a] site involved reconstructing the monument from whatever signs of its presence could still be recognised.
>
> (Thomas 2000: 86)

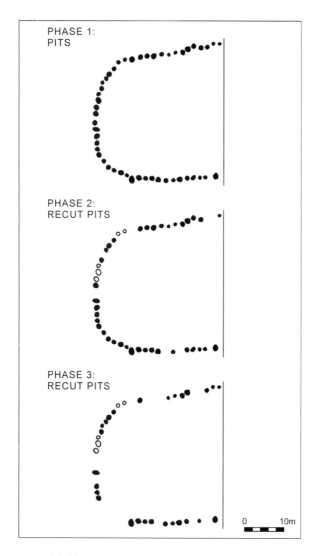

Figure 4.1 The structural sequence in the terminal of a Neolithic cursus at
Bannockburn, Scotland.

Source: information from Rideout (1997).

Where a timber structure had been burnt to the ground, its replacement
involved a number of factors: 'The monuments would have been reconstructed
through a combination of a memory of what had been there, the remaining traces
of the posts, and a particular understanding of the way in which the structure
had to be used' (ibid.: 86). Thomas refers specifically to structures built of earth
and stone and suggests that these would have been especially durable. Timber

constructions, on the other hand, had a finite life expectancy, even when they were left intact.

A similar point is made in a recent study by Parker Pearson and Ramilisonina (1998). They emphasise the distinctive sequence found in a number of cere-monial monuments of Neolithic and Early Bronze Age date in Britain, the most famous of which is Stonehenge. In many cases the first structure on the site was a timber circle, and this was often replaced by a similar arrangement of monoliths; there is little or no evidence for the opposite sequence, from stone to wood. The timber phases, they argue, are associated with quite extensive deposits of material culture, including food remains, decorated pottery and a series of distinctive artefacts. The stone circles that succeeded them show little of this evidence and often contain human bones. This division is a little too schematic – a few timber circles include cremation burials; timber and stone settings may have been combined at The Sanctuary and Mount Pleasant (Pollard 1992) – but their major point does seem to be correct. Monuments changed from an emphasis on the activities of the living to an association with the dead, just as they were built first of wood and then of stone. The latter distinction is important, for, like the human body, wood is subject to decay. Stone on the other hand, is virtually indestructible.

They compare this distinctive sequence with the construction of buildings in Madagascar, where a similar conceptual scheme has been identified, but their interpretation of the British evidence does not depend on this analogy – it is strong enough to stand on its own terms. One part of their case is especially interesting here. *Neolithic monuments change their form in a predetermined sequence.* They are constructed in timber and then they are rebuilt in stone, after which they are usually abandoned. Parker Pearson and Ramilisonina are especially interested in the symbolic meaning of this development, but another way of considering this kind of sequence is to suggest that such monuments were always intended to have a finite history and that their transformation had to follow a course that was laid down in advance. The remains of those monuments would still be visible to later generations, but again that is very different from the idea that such sites would remain unchanged for ever. Perhaps the successive transformations of timber circles formed part of the very rituals that were conducted there.

Rather than treat these processes separately, the present account will consider the distinctive nature of the sequence at a number of sites which were in use over roughly the same period of time (approximately 2500–2000 BC). Indeed, these separate sites came to resemble one another in their final forms, although each had undergone a quite different history of development. By the Late Neolithic/ Early Bronze Age, however, all included stone circles, and in every case these were the last major structures to be built there. Each of the sites is in Scotland. Machrie Moor is on the Isle of Arran on the west coast, Balnuaran of Clava is on the northern mainland and Tomnaverie is in the north-east of the country.

I have chosen to compare these specific sites for several reasons. All three have been recently excavated, two of them by the writer. Each shows a detailed history of construction extending over a finite period, and, most important of all, these monuments are usually attributed to separate architectural traditions. It is the character of the sequence that is important here, not the precise forms that they take.

Two adjacent timber circles were excavated on Machrie Moor, although they form part of a larger complex (Haggarty 1991) (Figure 4.2). These particular structures were built on very different scales from one another. The simpler monument consisted of a single ring of uprights, while its counterpart contained two concentric circles of posts with a massive square setting at their centre. There was probably an entrance on the south-west, diametrically opposite the position

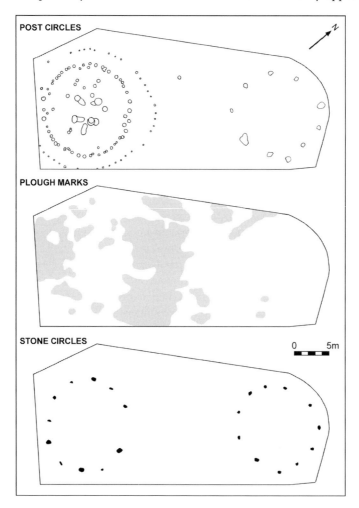

Figure 4.2 The structural sequence at Machrie Moor, Arran, Scotland.

Source: information from Haggarty (1991).

of the other circle. The principal monument has a very similar ground plan to the buildings found inside other ceremonial centres, but can also be considered as a massively enlarged version of the domestic buildings of the same period. Both the timber circles on Machrie Moor were associated with decorated pottery.

In between these two circles there was an upright post. This is important, for it seems to have been the only element of the original layout to be retained in a subsequent phase. The details are not clear-cut, but it appears that when both timber circles went out of use, the site was ploughed over. To judge from the ard marks recorded by the excavator, this must have happened on at least two separate occasions. During the same phase a number of stake fences were built across the positions of the older monuments, but these adopted different axes from the furrows, suggesting that these elements may not have been in use together. Ard marks were absent from the positions of the circles themselves, and this can be explained in more than one way. Haggarty considered that this was due to natural deterioration after these sites were uncovered during earlier work, but in fact the areas where this evidence is missing do not correspond to the limits of the previous excavation: it seems much more likely that the positions of the two timber settings were left untouched after the buildings themselves had decayed. There seems little reason to interpret this evidence in terms of everyday land use. Although cereal pollen was associated with the ard marks, the episode of cultivation may also have served to eradicate the traces of earlier activity on Machrie Moor. That would have had a similar effect to burning the timber structures inside cursuses.

One reason for taking this view is that once these episodes of cultivation were over the timber circles were replaced in precisely the same positions by two rings of standing stones. The excavator herself suggested that this could only have been achieved because the original layout of the site was still remembered, although the surviving wooden upright in between the two circles might have also have acted as a marker. Another reading of the field evidence is that the sites of the post-built monuments were indicated by small patches of unploughed land. At all events, the creation of the two stone circles reestablished the import-ance of these sites and did so in a much more durable form. After that time, no structural modifications were made to the monuments, although both of them were later used for cremation burials.

There are three points to emphasise here. Machrie Moor provides another instance of the familiar sequence from a timber monument to one built out of stone. The post circles are associated with a quantity of pottery, and the stone rings eventually contained Early Bronze Age burials. The two timber circles are of markedly different character from one another, and it may be significant that the more elaborate structure can be interpreted as an enormously enlarged version of the domestic buildings of the same period. By contrast, the stone settings that replaced them were virtually identical to one another.

At the same time, the succession from timber to stone was by no means straightforward. There were at least two episodes of cultivation in between these structural phases, and this activity may have served to cleanse the site before it changed its character. At least seven different fence lines are attributed to that phase, yet few of these follow the same alignments as the ard furrows, suggesting a significant break between the abandonment of the timber circles and their replacement in stone. This is much more akin to the cyclical destruction and replacement of monuments found at other sites in Scotland.

Lastly, it seems as if this sequence was preordained, in the sense that people had always been aware that the timber circles would eventually be replicated in stone, even if the site was cleared of any significant structures some time before that happened. It also seems likely that the creation of the stone circles was always intended as the final stage in the history of these monuments, even though they may have been reused for burying the dead.

In some ways this sequence is like that suggested by Parker Pearson and Ramilisonina, but in one respect it is rather different, for here an interval of uncertain duration separated the two phases of circle building. During that time all trace of the older structures was removed, so that the there was little but human memory to influence the final configuration of these monuments.

Similar considerations apply to other short-lived sites. For example, the Clava Cairns of Northern Scotland may have gone through a comparable history (Bradley 2000). At Machrie Moor the starting point for the sequence included a large timber setting whose ground plan seems to have been modelled on that of a late Neolithic house. At Balnuaran of Clava the results of excavation and environmental analysis suggest that a cemetery of megalithic cairns was built on the site of an older settlement

As their name suggests, the Clava Cairns are very different structures from the timber and stone settings described so far, for their most striking elements are a series of circular rubble enclosures (ring cairns) and passage graves (Figure 4.3). Each is surrounded by a circle of monoliths which increase in height towards the south-west and which may be directed towards the position of the summer moon. It has never been clear how these separate structures were related to one another, but recent excavation has provided some of the answers.

The cemetery at Balnuaran of Clava was built in an existing clearing with evidence for cereal cultivation. At least three of the individual monuments seem to incorporate substantial quantities of reused stonework, including a few pieces that were already decorated; since the latter were employed in building the corbels of two passage graves, the carved motifs were effectively hidden from view. Perhaps these came from existing structures on the site, and there is certainly evidence that another Clava Cairn had been built over the remains of a house (Simpson 1996). The removal of such a building might be compared with the destruction of the timber circles on Machrie Moor.

The cairns that were built at Balnuaran of Clava had a distinctive feature that they share with other sites of this kind: an emphasis on the south-west. In this particular case it is illustrated by the way in which the kerbstones retaining the edges of these monuments were graded in height. This meant that the cairns

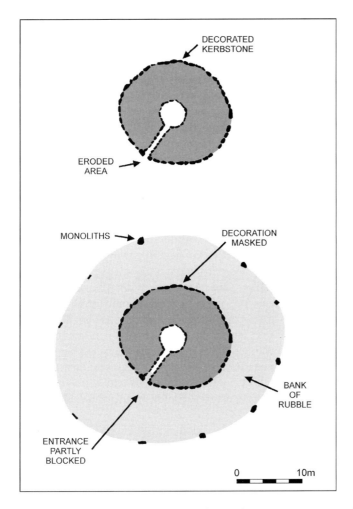

DECORATED
KERBSTONE

ERODED
AREA

MONOLITHS

DECORATION
MASKED

BANK
OF
RUBBLE

ENTRANCE
PARTLY
BLOCKED

0   10m

Figure 4.3 The structural sequence at the north-east passage grave at Balnuaran of
         Clava, Scotland.

would have been unstable. Unless the kerbstones had adequate foundations, the
smallest would have been pushed out of position as the core of the structure
began to settle.

That happened on other sites of this kind, but at Balnuaran of Clava large
sections of the kerb remained intact because they were buttressed by a bank of
rubble built up against the exterior of the monuments. This had to be built soon
after the kerb was erected, and yet there is evidence that an interval elapsed
between the construction of these different features. Individual kerbstones bore
carved decoration that would have been hidden from view when these external
banks were added, and there is evidence that the ground surface at the entrance

to one of the passage graves had been slightly lowered by erosion before that happened. Moreover, the construction of an external platform to retain the kerb made access to the burial chambers difficult, if not impossible.

The importance of this sequence is that it also involved the construction of stone circles. These rings of monoliths marked the edge of the rubble platforms built around the two passage graves and also defined an open area surrounding the ring cairn at Balnuaran of Clava. In the case of the passage graves it seems as if the stone circles were built at the same time as these additions were made to the monuments. That means that when the chambered cairns were enlarged and possibly closed, they were ringed by settings of upright stones.

That was not a fortuitous development. The stones making up these circles are graded in the same manner as the edges of the separate cairns, and individual monoliths are paired with the nearest element in the kerb through the careful selection of the raw material according to shape or colour. It is as if the building of the outer circle completed a plan that had been established from the outset. This is even more obvious in the case of the excavated ring cairn at Balnuaran of Clava, for here several of the monoliths were linked to its outer kerb by a bank of rubble. In one case that same alignment continued as a radial division that separated different deposits within the solid core of the monument. In each case, then, it seems as if the erection of a stone circle represented the completion of a plan that was played out over time, and as the perimeter of the monuments was demarcated by a ring of upright stones access to the burial chambers was closed. The difficulty of maintaining such unstable structures means that this sequence must have taken place over a short period of time. Like the stone circles on Machrie Moor, these monuments were reused for further burials, but the separate structures were never changed.

A similar sequence has been identified at another kind of monument which is often compared with Clava Cairns. Recumbent stone circles are found in North-East Scotland and have three main elements (Burl 2000: chapter 12). Like some of the sites just described, they consist of ring cairns enclosed by graded stone circles. Again the sites are aligned towards the south-west and the individual monoliths increase in height on that side of the circle. The main difference is that the two tallest stones (the 'flankers') bracket an enormous horizontal block (the 'recumbent'). Excavation on one such site, at Tomnaverie, has defined a structural sequence very similar to that at Balnuaran of Clava (Bradley *et al.* 2000) (Figure 4.4).

In this case the starting point for the sequence was a cremation pyre rather than a settlement. It was located in a prominent position on the end of a low ridge. The position of the pyre was incorporated into a massive platform which remained open at the centre where the surface of the hill outcropped. Like the cairns at Balnuaran of Clava, this structure was retained by a kerb, buttressed by a bank of rubble, but in this case the two features were built simultaneously. There were a number of radial divisions in the structure of this cairn, linking points in the interior to stones in the outer kerb. The effect was to embellish the position of the

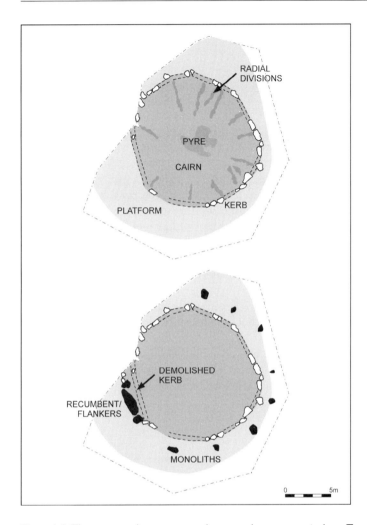

Figure 4.4 The structural sequence at the recumbent stone circle at Tomnaverie, Scotland.

pyre and to extend the level surface of the hilltop towards the south-west where it commanded a view towards a distant mountain (Lochnagar), 30 kilometres away.

In common with the other examples, the last development at Tomnaverie was the construction of a stone circle. This enclosed the existing cairn, and the recumbent stone was manoeuvred into position on top of the bank of rubble that had held its kerb in place. One section of the monument was rebuilt to join the edge of the existing platform to the positions of the flankers. This focused the view from the monument on a narrower area until it was directed towards the position of the moon approximately once every generation.

Again the sequence at Tomnaverie seems to have followed a preordained plan, so that the successive phases of use and construction may have been important elements in the rituals that were conducted there. The location of the cremation pyre was not selected at random, for it occupied the only position on the hilltop which commanded a view of the moon as it passed over Lochnagar. The construction of the cairn emphasised that alignment and extended the surface of the hilltop towards the south-west. Again the structure of the cairn seems to have been conceived in the knowledge that a stone circle would eventually be built there. The longest straight section of kerb was precisely where the recumbent and flankers would be located, and a number of the radial divisions built into the fabric of the cairn were directed towards the positions where upright stones would be raised. It is easy to suggest that the work proceeded continuously, but that is hardly likely since the creation of the stone circle necessitated the demolition of a massive section of kerb and its reconstruction in a different position. Again the sequence seems to have unfolded over a period of time. The fact that the monument is aligned on the moon once every 18½ years may give some indication of the interval, or intervals, involved (Ruggles 1999: chapter 5 and 212–15).

Like the other sites discussed in this section, the erection of the stone circle at Tomnaverie brought the sequence to an end, although it was later reused for burial. All three monuments seem to have been built according to a plan that may have been laid down from the beginning, so that each successive structure had its place in the unfolding of a ritual that extended over a finite period of time. It may be that the cycle would be repeated on other sites, but that is simply conjecture. At all events, the construction of a stone circle may have closed the monument to the living and brought these projects to an end.

Aosta

In other cases the sequence may have extended over a longer period, so it would not have been as easy to lay down the procedures that later generations should follow. In Chapter 2 I considered the distinctive character of the archaeological sequence at Petit Chasseur. I would now like to discuss some rather similar evidence from Aosta in Northern Italy (de Marinis 1995; Mezzena 1998b).

Like Petit Chasseur, the site at Aosta was well preserved because it was contained within a deep sequence of deposits. It was also associated with a number of radiocarbon dates, although these are not always consistent with the stratified sequence; where there is any disagreement, this account will follow the excavator's interpretation of the stratigraphy (Mezzena 1998b). The monuments are laid out along a slight ridge running from north-east to south-west. This is important as it seems to have established the axis for almost all the monuments, whose history extends for approximately a millennium, from about 3000 to 2000 BC.

In its early stages the history of the site shows a striking resemblance to that of the Scottish monuments (Figure 4.5). The earliest structure at Aosta was a line of

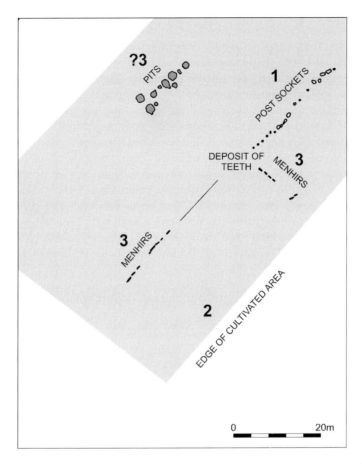

Figure 4.5 The original layout of the monument complex at Aosta, Northern Italy.
Source: information from Mezzena (1998b).

massive stone-packed posts which followed the contours and formed two slight arcs running from north-east to south-west. These uprights may have been erected over a considerable time, but this cannot be proved. The associated radiocarbon dates certainly span a significant period. They fall into two groups, but their age ranges seem to depend mainly on which laboratory had processed the samples. The post sockets were associated with a number of placed deposits, including ashes and cattle skulls. Like the circle at Tomnaverie, the post alignment may have been directed towards the moon. It established an axis that was to influence all the later structures at Aosta. It is impossible to tell the original forms of these uprights, but the fact that the same alignment was to be continued by a row of statue menhirs suggests that they may originally have been carved and might even have represented human figures.

Despite this obvious relationship, there can be little question of direct continuity between the timber and stone settings. Like the excavated area on Machrie Moor, the entire site at Aosta seems to have been ploughed. This eradicated the traces of some of the wooden uprights and seems to have predated the erection of any of the stone settings. Cultivation took place over most of the site.

There is reason to believe that the cultivated area had a special significance. It respected part of the existing post setting and followed its alignment, but another section may have been destroyed. This episode of ploughing post-dated the earliest wooden uprights by approximately 250 years, but it also established the area in which stone structures were soon to be built. There is no evidence of an adjacent settlement, and once again the transformation of the site may have been intended to cleanse it before further developments could happen there. One reason for taking this view is that a limited area just beyond the end of the post setting had been 'sown' with human teeth, particularly incisors. This is among the earliest evidence of ploughing to be found anywhere in Italy, and the odd association with teeth, which echoes the Classical story of Jason, cannot be understood in practical terms.

The next development at Aosta also recalls the Scottish evidence, for again the timber structure was replaced in stone. Two alignments of anthropomorphic sculptures were created once the phase of ploughing was over. One extended the row first established by the timber setting, and the second ran at right angles to this line. Both groups of stones converged in the area with the deposit of human teeth. Again the chronology of these statues presents some problems, as it is not known whether they were erected piecemeal or whether each setting was created fully formed. In one case two neighbouring statues are so similar to one another that they may have been conceived as part of a more general plan, and in another instance three examples shared the same foundation trench. Unlike their timber predecessors, the menhirs were not associated with any offerings. On the other hand, their construction does seem to be linked with that of two platforms. Beneath one of these was a deposit of human bones.

Elsewhere on the site there was a row of pits. This ran parallel to the main alignment of menhirs and was located directly opposite the other row of sculptures. The chronological position of these pits is a little uncertain, but they had been cut through the layer of ploughsoil and were most probably contemporary with the earlier of the stone settings. Each of these pits had been filled in a highly structured manner, with alternating layers of material obtained from two different levels in the subsoil. They contained burnt cereals and a consistent range of artefacts, among which there were querns and distinctive pairs of natural stones, one a rounded pebble and the other a flat piece of schist of triangular or polygonal outline. Neither of them were formal artefacts but this association was repeated sufficiently often for the pattern to be significant. In some ways the small slabs may have been regarded as miniature versions of the menhirs, which were made out of similar materials. In that case we could compare the careful burial of these pieces with the erection – or, perhaps, the levelling – of the decorated stones.

Several points need emphasising here. Despite the episode of ploughing which may have cleansed the site of its previous associations, the principal stone alignment continued the course of the one made out of wood. In doing so, it could have perpetuated the lunar orientation of the original monuments at Aosta. The same applies to the line of pits that has just been described. At the same time, each successive phase was associated with specialised deposits: cattle skulls were placed beneath the wooden posts, teeth were scattered over a limited area of the ploughsoil, and human bones were buried under a platform associated with the statue menhirs. Agricultural symbolism was obviously important, and there may be links between the ploughing of the site and the deposits of quernstones and cereals that were buried during the following phase.

How were those statues organised on the site? They were laid out in two rows, with the individual images facing in the same direction so as to create a screen. The sculptures were more or less life size and would have been brightly coloured when they were newly carved. All of them depicted the human figure. It is not possible to distinguish between men and women, but there do seem to be two main groups of sculptures based upon details of costume and associated artefacts. They had occasionally been altered, suggesting that individual examples may have been standing for a significant period of time. Two distinctive styles of stone carving have been identified at Aosta, both of which depict recognisable types of ornaments and weapons. These comparisons lend some support to the idea that the more elaborate statues may be later than the others.

Once they had been erected, the statues seem to have shared a common history. They were deliberately damaged, particularly around the shoulders and head, and then they were taken down. Although it would have been possible to remove them from their sockets, people preferred to break them off at ground level, so that the bottom part of each stone remained in place. Sometimes the remainder of the statue was left where it had fallen. Many of these pieces were reused during a later phase, but the excavator suggests that the lower portions of the stones were left in position to preserve the memory of the original settings.

Fragments of these sculptures were incorporated into mortuary monuments on the same site (Figure 4.6). The largest and perhaps most striking of these was a megalithic tomb associated with a low triangular cairn very similar to those at Petit Chasseur (Gallay 1995). At Aosta, this was located on the axis of the principal row of menhirs, midway between the two stone platforms with which they were associated. Four further tombs, two of them roughly circular, were erected during this phase, but these structures have not survived so well. The largest of them continued the axis created by the stone sculptures, the two platforms and the triangular cairn, but the others depart from that design. This small group of tombs also extended beyond the area that had been ploughed. All these monuments date from the end of the third millennium BC, and the building of the triangular cairn is associated with Bell Beaker pottery. Three of the newly built monuments incorporate the remains of statues.

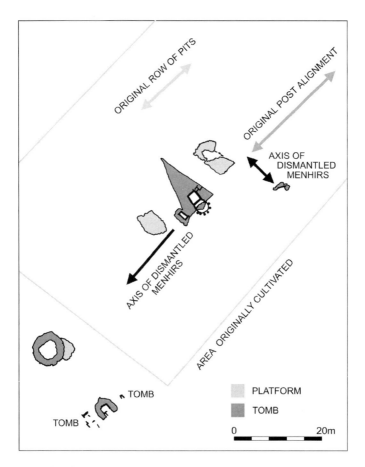

ORIGINAL ROW OF PITS

ORIGINAL POST ALIGNMENT

AXIS OF
DISMANTLED
MENHIRS

AXIS OF DISMANTLED
MENHIRS

AREA ORIGINALLY CULTIVATED

TOMB

TOMB

PLATFORM

TOMB

0   20m

Figure 4.6 Subsequent modifications to the layout of the monument complex at Aosta,
Northern Italy.

Source: information from Mezzena (1998b).

In the final phase of activity at Aosta, three monumental cists were constructed, all of them within the area that had already been defined by cultivation. Each
is directly related to elements of the existing layout. Two of these cists abut the
triangular cairn, while the remaining example was located on the axis of the
shorter row of menhirs. These monuments also belong to the end of the third
millennium. Again their structure incorporates substantial fragments of the
earlier sculptures. One feature of interest is that during the final period of activity,
people seem to have decided to reuse some of the older statues, instead of the
more elaborately carved pieces employed during the previous phase.

The three Scottish stone circles considered earlier provided examples of
projects where the structural sequence may have been preordained. It extended

through a prescribed series of events, and when they were complete each of the sites was closed. In every case the creation of a ring of monoliths seems to have brought their immediate history to an end. There were obvious indications of how each building should develop, and it may be that these were actually built into its structure from the beginning. There do not seem to have been any radical departures from that plan, and each sequence may have ended after a relatively short period of time.

Aosta is a rather different case. I doubt whether any of the Scottish monuments were used for very long, but the history of this site extends over a millennium. Certain elements do seem to have been respected throughout. For the most part, the monuments are arranged along an alignment that runs from north-east to south-west, and in this case it may be related to the position of the moon. That alignment follows the lie of the land but it also forms a connection between the original file of wooden uprights, the main row of statue menhirs, the pits with deposits of quernstones and the position of a megalithic tomb. Moreover, it was reinforced by the ploughing of the site before its translation from a timber monument to one built out of stone. But it would be easy to exaggerate the importance of these observations, for in other respects those conventions were breaking down towards the end of the sequence. Only two of the earlier group of megaliths still conformed to the initial design, and four out of five of these monuments were actually outside the area that had been defined by ploughing. In the phase that followed, three monumental cists were built at Aosta, but only one of these was really related to the original layout of the site. This was positioned on the course of one of the lines of menhirs, but the other two monuments referred no further back than the triangular cairn built during the previous phase. By this time it seems possible that people no longer understood the history of the site. At Petit Chasseur, fragments of older sculptures were built into a series of tombs, but this sequence of reuse ran in parallel with the order in which these carvings had been made, so that the oldest fragments were the first to be incorporated into these monuments, while pieces of the later menhirs were employed in the next generation of structures. The opposite happened at Aosta *where the newer sculptures were reused first and the oldest statues were built into the fabric of the latest monuments on the site.* That might have been an explicit reference to the history of these particular pieces – akin to the careful preservation of the stumps of levelled sculptures – but it is just as likely that the original intentions behind the creation of this complex had been forgotten (Table 4.1).

I have compared this sequence of development with that at Petit Chasseur, for there are obvious similarities in the character of both these sites. Yet in another respect they differ from one another. Petit Chasseur was used for a variety of secondary burials well into the Early Bronze Age, although the recycling of statues came to an end (Gallay 1995). Perhaps the ideas that had led to the creation of these complexes finally lost their power. Whereas Aosta seems to have been abandoned after a phase in which the original design had broken down, Petit Chasseur makes the same point in a different way. It continued to

Table 4.1   The archaeological sequence at Aosta according to Mezzena (1998b) emphasising the references to the past made in Phases 1–3, and (in italics) the ways in which developments in Phase 4 depart from the original design

Phase	Main structures	Relationship to the past
1	File of wooden uprights (?originally carved)	Uprights conform to lunar alignment
2	Cultivation and sowing of human teeth	Cultivated area reflects the alignment of the wooden uprights
3	Erection of statue menhirs	One row continues the alignment of the wooden uprights
3?	Excavation of pits	The row of pits runs parallel to the main alignment of menhirs
4	Damage to menhirs, followed by dismantling. Incorporation of broken menhirs into tombs	*Some tombs depart from the original axis of the site. The cemetery extends beyond the area originally cultivated. The menhirs are not reused in the sequence in which they were made*

play an important role, but now it was just one of a series of Bronze Age cemeteries, and the first part of its history may no longer have mattered to the people who used the site. This may have happened because events could no longer be recalled, but it is just as likely that the later use of Petit Chasseur expressed a quite different understanding of its importance. That could have come about through a conscious process of reinterpretation. I shall explore both possibilities in the last part of this chapter through an account of the changing uses of Neolithic monuments in North-West France.

Carnac

Again this account is closely related to my discussion in Chapter 2 where I considered the complicated relationship between decorated standing stones and megalithic tombs. There, I was concerned with the earliest monuments in Southern Brittany: menhirs, long mounds and passage graves. Now I would like to follow the sequence over a longer period.

This study is not concerned with the archaeology of the entire region, but with a limited area around Carnac in the Morbihan, for it is here that the greatest concentration of monuments is found. To some extent that may be deceptive, as the majority of these sites were located in a zone of raised ground overlooking a large area which has now been lost to the sea. Although certain sites are partly submerged, in particular the famous stone settings of Er Lannic (Le Rouzic 1930), it is not clear that the lowlands had ever contained the same density of structures. In fact it seems more likely that the primary focus of monument building was an inland area whose southern limit was eventually bounded by a series of four alignments of standing stones (Bailloud *et al.* 1995).

It is a region with a wide range of monument types but an archaeological sequence that lacks much chronological precision. That was because until quite recently these structures had been considered separately from one another, so that each type of building was classified and dated as an independent exercise. This is no longer true, but it is still quite uncommon for discussion of the archaeological evidence to consider the landscape as a whole. The situation is unfortunate, as some of the problems are diminished when the relationships between separate structures are considered on a larger scale. In particular, it allows us to consider the creation and use of newly built monuments in relation to the earlier history of this region. As seems to have happened at Aosta, any attempt to prescribe how these structures would be understood seems to have been defeated by the ways in which successive generations interpreted the monuments of the past.

In the Carnac region the variety of separate types of monuments can seem quite bewildering: menhirs, long mounds, 'grands tumulus', passage graves, enclosures and alignments (Bailloud *et al.* 1995). Few of these are found in stratigraphic relationship to one another, and fewer still are associated with reliable radiocarbon dates. On the other hand, this sheer diversity suggests that the sequence was particularly volatile. Like Kafka's Great Wall of China, the meanings of these different monuments seem to have extended well beyond the intentions of those who built them.

I have already considered the early years of this sequence, but now it is necessary to look at them in more detail. In Chapter 2 I argued that decorated menhirs were systematically related to the early long mounds of Southern Brittany and that they were sometimes broken up and incorporated in the first passage graves. Similar processes could be recognised elsewhere in Atlantic Europe and so it seemed unlikely that this practice resulted from the conflict between indigenous hunter-gatherers and settlers from the east. Now it is important to consider two other kinds of evidence. First, it seems as if some of the early long mounds were greatly enlarged to form the *grands tumulus* which are such a distinctive feature of the Carnac region (Figure 4.7). There is disagreement over when this happened (Patton 1993: chapter 5; Boujot and Cassen 1998), but it still seems likely that it was accomplished before the building of passage graves against the flanks of these mounds. The second problem is raised by the presence of a stone row beside one of these earthworks at Locmariaquer. All but one of the uprights were removed when a passage grave, La Table des Marchand, was erected on the same site, and yet it has been conventional to date the major alignments in this region to the *Later* Neolithic. That may be unsatisfactory, as another Breton stone setting, Les Pierres droites, is associated with radiocarbon dates in the early part of this period (Lecerf 1999). It seems likely that the building of these structures was a long lived tradition.

The most striking feature of the Carnac region is the great concentration of

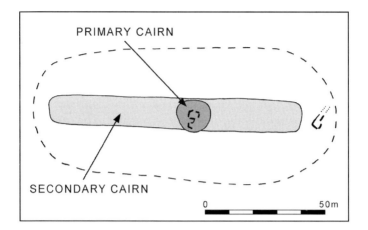

Figure 4.7 The structural sequence at Tumulus Mont Saint-Michel, Carnac, Brittany.

Source: information from Le Rouzic (1932).

Note
The dashed line indicates the extent of the final mound.

different kinds of monument on the higher ground overlooking what was once the coastal plain. Towards the southern limit of this distribution four stone alignments cross an area of higher ground between two valleys (Figure 4.8). Although there are some exceptions, the great majority of the monuments are found along the course of this division or in the area to its north. At the same time, the Carnac alignments provide a kind of datum to which the other monuments can be related (Bailloud *et al.* 1995).

Not only do they mark the southern limit of the distribution of long mounds and decorated menhirs, they actually incorporate examples of both these monuments. The Kermanio alignment, for example, take its axis from an existing long mound (Le Manio) and incorporates it into its path (Figure 4.9). Moreover, the stone setting was organised so as to include the position of a decorated menhir that was already present on the site. The Kerlesan stone avenue continues the axis of a similar mound, although the two are not superimposed, and beyond its limits there is a third example which shares the same orientation. The sequence at Le Manio would certainly suggest that such mounds were among the first monuments to be built, in which case their distinctive configuration was emphasised on a spectacular scale by the erection of the standing stones. The same explanation might apply to the building of the *grands tumulus*, for some of these are massively enlarged long barrows. One of the sites, Tumulus St Michel, is located to the south of the Carnac stone rows and overlooks the alignment at Le Ménec (Le Rouzic 1932). The two structures are laid out roughly parallel to one another. Again excavation has shown that the tumulus was built over a less conspicuous long mound or *tertre tumulaire*.

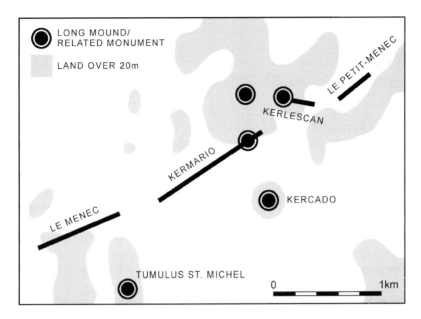

Figure 4.8 An outline plan of the Carnac alignments, emphasising their relationship to higher ground and their juxtaposition with long mounds and related monuments. The enclosed passage grave at Kercado is also shown.

Source: information from Bailloud *et al.* (1995).

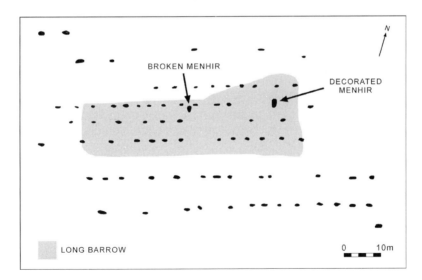

Figure 4.9 The relationship between the long barrow with its decorated menhir at Le Manio, Brittany, and the course of the later stone alignment.

Source: information from Bailloud *et al.* (1995).

The four major alignments at Carnac – Kermanio, Kerlescan Le Ménec and Le Petit-Ménec – are directly related to other kinds of monument. It seems likely that they led between the distinctive stone enclosures that are sometimes described as *cromlechs* (Bailloud *et al.* 1995). These structures can be dated in two ways. In one case, at Kerlescan, a cromlech adopts an existing tertre tumulaire as one of its boundaries, and the stone perimeter abuts each end of the mound (Figure 4.10). Again the enclosure should post-date the construction of this earthwork: a relationship which recalls that between the alignment and the long mound of Le Manio. There is also some dating evidence from the badly excavated site of Er Lannic where two cromlechs survive as free-standing structures. These seem to have been associated with deposits of decorated pottery of a type that is normally dated to around 4000 BC (Le Rouzic 1930). That would be consistent with the date of some of the passage graves that incorporate fragments of older menhirs. One of these was at Kercado, close to the Kermanio alignment. This is interesting for two reasons. It was roofed by a reused menhir, decorated with a carving of an axe head, and the cairn itself was enclosed within a setting of upright stones built in the same manner as a cromlech (L'Helgouac'h 1965: figure 7).

There is some evidence that this complex built up gradually over time. It has long been observed that as the stones in the different rows approached the enclosures at their terminals they seemed to have changed their character. The monoliths became significantly taller than those in the other sections of the avenue, yet there is also some evidence that this scheme lost definition over time. At the western end of the Le Ménec alignment, there is a large oval enclosure, which seems to have had a single opening to the east. Burl has argued that this was originally approached by just two rows of standing stones (1993: 134–46). These are quite distinct from the other monoliths because they run precisely parallel to one another and are aligned on that entrance (Figure 4.11). Moreover,

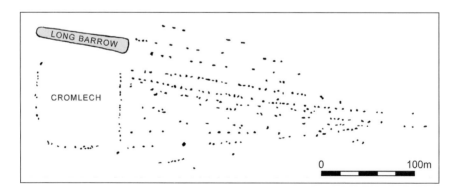

Figure 4.10 The relationship between a long barrow, a cromlech and the stone alignment at Kerlescan, Carnac.

Source: information from Bailloud *et al.* (1995).

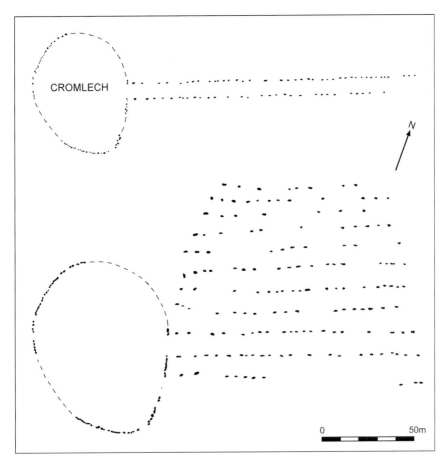

Figure 4.11 The original design of the Ménec West cromlech and its subsequent
modification, according to the interpretation proposed by Burl (1993).

they increase steadily in height towards the position of the enclosure. Yet there
are as many as ten other stone rows in this particular setting, the majority of
which stop short of the cromlech itself. In fact, five of them are not even aligned
on the position of the enclosure and, had their course been extended, they would
have missed it altogether.

There are other anomalous features in the Carnac alignments. It is clear that
the monuments were originally conceived according to a fairly straightforward
plan and that separate sections might have involved the collection of raw material
from different kinds of surface deposit (Sellier 1995). Yet, on a more detailed
level, the distinctive form of the alignments is lost. It is not quite clear how many
different rows of stones were built and their axes occasionally cut across one
another. Many of the individual files of monoliths can be divided into shorter

sections, each made up of stones of roughly the same size, as if they had been built by a single work force and had been chosen because these were the largest pieces that they could manoeuvre into position. Often those separate sections were subtly misaligned, adding to the impression that construction was episodic and may have taken place over a long period. The number of separate rows could have increased with time until some of them may no longer have been directed towards the positions of the cromlechs. The separate alignments may also have been lengthened. In each case the effect would have been the same: the original design was obscured as the project developed a momentum of its own. Once the last monoliths were in place any relationship with earlier long barrows had been largely lost (Table 4.2).

Indeed, by that stage the local population was engaged in building a new generation of monuments in the Carnac landscape. The distribution of passage graves in the Morbihan is significantly wider than that of long barrows and decorated menhirs, although the earliest of the chambered tombs incorporated older stone carvings in their fabric. Only one of the passage graves was physically connected to the alignments, and for the most part the stone rows simply marked the southern edge of a much wider distribution of monuments (Boujot and Cassen 1998). That remained the case with later forms of chambered cairn, including angled passage graves and allées couvertes.

To sum up, the first generation of monuments in this region seem to have been the long barrows and decorated menhirs. Both appear to have been the subject of considerable attention during subsequent phases. The connection between them depends on the ways in which the sculpted stones were reused in the structure of early passage graves. This formed part of a much wider pattern and may represent the culmination of a ritual played out by monument building, not unlike that described in earlier sections of this chapter. At the same time, both the original elements in the Carnac landscape were elaborated in another way. The positions of the long barrows were emphasised in a more arresting form through the construction of mounds and stone rows. Some of the tertres tumulaires with their closed cist burials were massively enlarged to form the grands tumulus which are

Table 4.2 An interpretation of the archaeological sequence at Carnac

Original conception	Monumental elaboration
Long mounds	Mounds enlarged to form 'Carnac tumuli'
	Passage graves built against flanks
	Long axis extended by stone rows
	Long axis overridden by stone rows
	Long axis forms one side of stone enclosure (cromlech)
Menhirs	Decorated menhir incorporated in later stone row
	Broken fragments built into passage graves
	Number of rows increased over time?
	Lengths of rows increased over time?

such a striking feature of this region of Brittany, while the positions of others were reinforced by the construction of stone settings which perpetuated their original alignments. These might lead towards, or even across, the older earth-works. The statue menhirs associated with such mounds were celebrated in another way, too. In many cases they were broken up and incorporated in a new generation of monuments, but at Le Manio one of these was actually incor-porated into a new configuration of standing stones. This is of especial interest in the light of the recent observation that the early site of Les Pierres droites, in the interior of the country, may have included menhirs that had been shaped to resemble the human body (Lecerf 1999). Perhaps the separate monoliths in the Carnac alignments were originally conceived as memorials to particular individuals. This link between the tertres tumulaires and the stone rows goes even further in fact, for these settings extend between the series of stone enclosures described as cromlechs, and the site at Kerlescan uses an existing long barrow as one of its boundaries (Bailloud *et al.* 1995: 56–8).

These may be some of the elements that made up the original scheme at Carnac, but over the course of time those simple outlines were compromised, as often as not by the sheer scale of the project. More and more stones were added to the alignments until their original axis was obscured, and in the end even their relationship to the cromlechs was affected. Some of the individual files of mono-liths drifted off course or cut across one another, while others no longer led to these great stone enclosures at all. The more elaborate the alignments became, the harder it would have been to understand their critical relationship to the long barrows that were there before them.

The creation of so many elaborate monuments in this small area brought about other changes. The tertres tumulaires had been closed structures that no one could enter once the cists beneath them had been sealed, and yet they were replaced by entirely permeable stone settings and by great open-air arenas. The individual menhirs that had been connected with these mounds were eclipsed by the enormous number of monoliths that were erected in succeeding phases, and, if the standing stones indeed stood for particular people in the past, their signifi-cance would have been lost in a crowd of other images. Indeed, it even seems possible that some of the stone settings incorporated basic celestial alignments (ibid.: 45–6), so that their significance extended beyond the local landscape altogether and took in the positions of the sun and moon. By this stage, the sites of individual long mounds may not have seemed important. The very nature of monumental architecture had changed.

A summary

In this chapter I have considered the notion that monuments were intended as memorials, for in that way their builders may have tried to dictate how future generations would perceive the past: these buildings could have been attempts to formulate the memories of the future. In some cases that may have been what was intended, but there are other sites which look just as 'monumental' that were not meant to have this effect at all, and in these cases they were supposed to be used over a shorter period. Indeed, the people who constructed them seem to have envisaged the time when the use of these places would cease. There is almost endless variation in the archaeological record. If Machrie Moor, Balnuaran of Clava and Tomnaverie were supposed to be used over a finite period, any such scheme for the use of the monuments at Aosta seems to have broken down at quite an early stage. At Carnac, the oldest monuments in the landscape were eventually obscured by the very structures that were intended to celebrate them. The builders lost touch with the original aims of the project, and the process of monument building seems to have taken on a life of its own.

Many of the same problems were identified by Kafka in *The Great Wall of China*. There may never have been a consensus over why monuments were built or the ideas they were supposed to convey to later generations. Such projects may have had many different starting points, and only a few of them may have reached a definite conclusion. There was always the possibility of changing the original plan – of building a new Tower of Babel on top of a defensive wall – and it may never have been completely clear how far such building programmes had a practical aim in view and how far they played a less overt political role. Indeed, Kafka's story shows how difficult it is to be sure of the audience towards which such lavish efforts were directed.

It was even less likely that the original building project could actually achieve the aims that are suggested by the word 'monument'. Such constructions might serve to remind later generations of what had gone before, but they could not enforce a single interpretation of the past. The characters in Kafka's story are loyal to the Chinese emperor, but news travels so slowly that they do not know which emperor to obey or which orders remained in force. They have to make their own way among so much confusing information.

Part of the problem concerns the relationship between memory and time. Some of the monuments, characterised by Machrie Moor, Tomnaverie and Clava, were used over quite a short period. Either the structures were destroyed and renewed in a more durable medium, or the design of the monument un-folded over a few years before these buildings were completed and abandoned. The passage graves at Balnuaran of Clava were orientated on an annual event, the mid winter sunset, and the stone circle at Tomnaverie was directed towards the position of the summer moon approximately once every 18 years. Because such sequences were quite short, it would have been easy to adhere to a single plan, and the meanings of these monuments should have remained unaltered. It seems likely that the practises associated with these sites adhered to a simple rhythm, punctuated by the movement of the heavenly bodies and the passage of human generations.

The same may have been true of the earlier stages in the use of Aosta and Carnac. At Aosta, the initial alignment of wooden uprights was again directed towards the moon, and it seems possible that it had always been intended to replace these post with menhirs. In the same way, I argued in Chapter 2 that such statues were also meant to have a finite history before they were broken up and incorporated in other monuments – that interpretation might apply to both these sites. But as these places were used over a longer time, memories of their original design might have become unstable, as so often happens with oral traditions. It may have been less obvious how these rituals had originated, and for that reason each of the sites witnessed what were really quite new developments. This was rather less apparent at Aosta where the lunar axis of the structures retained some of its importance. At Carnac, however, an initial pattern of long barrows was elaborated on such a massive scale that the original significance of these places may have been completely obscured. The stone alignments could have taken these structures as their point of departure, but the evolution of the Carnac landscape suggests that the importance of the burial mounds was gradually forgotten. Again there is some evidence of shorter sequences within the grand design. These are best illustrated by the progressive additions to the stone rows, but the fact that so many of them depart from the basic plan suggests that its primary meanings were lost as new interpretations took their place. To some extent that resulted from the frailty of human memory over the longue durée, but it was at least as important that these places were being adapted to changing circumstances. Much the same seems to have happened in the transmission of epic poems (Morris 1986).

I have used Kafka's short story to encapsulate some of the paradoxes that affect the archaeology of monuments, but there is one last possibility to consider. People would have lived among the monuments of past generations and yet precise knowledge of the reasons for building them would very often have been lost. These buildings could have been modified to accommodate fresh interpretations of the world, and newer constructions could well have taken the place of older ones. But the sheer scale on which they had been made meant that they would never be completely absent from human consciousness. Just as they may once have been built to enshrine a particular system of belief, they could be reused and interpreted in a very different way, even if they had been abandoned for many years. Such ancient ruins exercise a special power over posterity. In Chapter 5 I must consider the archaeology practised in the past itself, for I shall discuss the ways in which people in prehistory interpreted the remains of antiquity and invested them with a new significance.

Chapter 5

Remaking ancient pasts
From revision to revival

INTERPRETATION, CONFRONTATION AND LEGITIMATION

Saint Protasus and Saint Gervaise

How is it possible for Christian saints to have lived in the Palaeolithic period? J. B. S. Haldane (1985) tells the story in his essay 'God-makers'.

The details are not entirely clear, but it seems as if some time in the fourth century AD the bones of two people were discovered beneath a church floor in Northern Italy. Their bodies had been covered with red ochre. The Bishop of Milan, Saint Ambrose, had a dream in which it was revealed that these were the remains of Christian martyrs who had been put to death by Nero. The relics soon proved to have miraculous powers, curing a blind man and expelling demons, and so the skeletons were canonised. Set free from their prehistoric context, they became Saint Protasus and Saint Gervaise.

More recent discoveries suggest that in fact both the bodies date from the Upper Palaeolithic, the earliest phase with a clearly defined burial rite in Europe. They are found in a region where such evidence is well documented, and the distinctive form of this deposit has obvious parallels in the Gravettian burials from the Grimaldi caves on the border between Italy and France (Gamble 1999: 405–9).

Saint Ambrose could not have been expected to know this. For him, the red ochre would have represented human lifeblood (as it may have done for Palaeolithic people), but that symbol was interpreted in a Christian context. His opinion was supported by the dream in which Protasus and Gervaise had been identified as martyrs. With the benefit of hindsight, it is easy to suggest that Ambrose may have made a mistake, but what he did was little different from the experience of anyone else confronted with archaeological evidence of an unfamiliar kind. Guided by the ideas current in his own society, he proposed an interpretation, and, as a result, the Upper Palaeolithic lost two of its burials and the church acquired two supernumerary saints.

This is an unusual example of a much more general phenomenon. People in the past will always have been confronted by the surviving remains of antiquity. These might be explained in many different ways: through documentary sources, through place names, through surviving oral traditions or simply by reference to the experience and expectations current at the time. Where the material in question was very ancient it is hardly surprising that this process should have given misleading results. It is unreasonable to expect anyone to have followed the procedures of archaeological enquiry before those methods were invented. Yet the very presence of so many reminders of a remote past in the experience of later generations did require some response. Even if those signs were ignored, that was a reaction in itself.

The case of the Palaeolithic saints is not an isolated instance. The Christian church found it difficult to come to terms with the pagan past. The relationship between these different systems of belief defines the issues clearly. Fortunately, there is some historical evidence relevant to the problem. Attitudes varied between confrontation and assimilation. At first, Christian communities were expected to destroy the relics of pagan belief, but later they were encouraged to incorporate them within the fabric of the new religion (Daniel 1972: 25). The first of these approaches is self-explanatory, but the second would have involved a process of reinterpretation. The adoption of Saint Protasus and Saint Gervaise is one example of this, although people could not have been aware of it at the time. The treatment of other prehistoric remains followed a similar course.

Christians and the pagan past

Two examples may be helpful here. Among the more obvious relics of the prehistoric past were rock art and megalithic tombs. Both were adapted in quite distinctive ways.

The treatment of megalithic tombs has been discussed many times, in particular by Daniel (1972). Churches might be built next to these sites, or the tombs themselves could be included within Christian cemeteries. In certain cases their surviving remains might even be incorporated inside ecclesiastical buildings. Thus the separate components of the prehistoric monuments might be dismantled and used as altars, or the structure could be left standing as a kind of chapel. Menhirs might be refashioned as open air crosses, and burial mounds could even be selected as the sites of Christian buildings. An obvious example was considered in the previous chapter: Tumulus St Michel at Carnac, where a church was built on top of an enormous barrow (Le Rouzic 1932).

In other cases the treatment of megaliths was more subtle and can only be investigated by excavation. A good example is the reuse of those monuments in Normandy described as allées couvertes (Billard et al. 1998). They were sometimes adopted as the sites of early Medieval cemeteries (Figure 5.1). This relationship has been investigated in a number of places, where it appears that at least parts of the Neolithic structure could still be recognised in the later first millennium AD. These ruined monuments became the focus for a new phase of

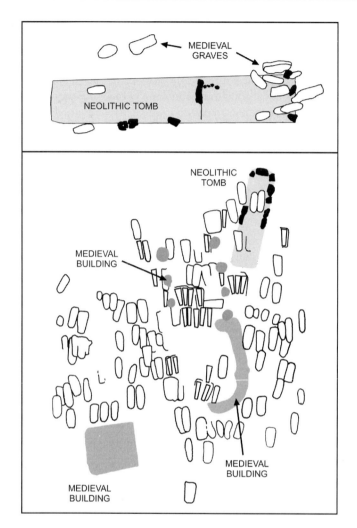

Figure 5.1 Neolithic tombs at Portjoie and Val-de-Reuil, Northern France, reused as
            Christian cemeteries.

Source: information from Billard, Carré and Treffort (1998).

activity, but it did not always take the same form. In certain cases it seems as if the
stonework of the Neolithic tombs was damaged or destroyed. At other sites, for
example Portejoie, the existing layout of the monuments was respected, so that
the Medieval graves clustered around the entrance of the burial chamber.

For the most part the Medieval burials were organised on an east–west axis
consistent with Christian practice, but at one of the excavated megaliths in
Normandy, Beausoleil 3, some of the graves adopted a north–south alignment
because they were dug along the flanks of the existing monument. On another

site, Butte-Saint-Cyr, where the Medieval burials shared an east–west alignment, there are signs of a still more complex sequence, beginning with the deliberate destruction of a Neolithic tomb and ending with the erection of a Christian church on the site. The entrance to that church was only 2 metres from the position of the prehistoric monument and both the structures shared the same orientation.

Such observations had been made in fieldwork for many years, but they had not been discussed in much detail until recently. Now it seems likely that such developments resulted from the initial impact of Christianity. Some monuments were destroyed while the remains of others were respected, but all these places were sanctified by a new generation of graves. That is consistent with the church's recommendations in the Codicil of the Synod of Nantes, although the age of that document is disputed (ibid.).

Similar edicts were issued in the north of Iberia where the local population was instructed to combat the pagan cult of rocks (Sanches *et al.* 1998: 93–4). No doubt this term included the use of chambered tombs, where Christian imagery was carved on the walls, but the main impact seems to have been on the treatment of open air rock art. This has had a serious consequence for modern research as it meant that many carved or painted outcrops gained a fresh generation of images. Often the new designs extended across the decorated surface, as if to provide a commentary on what was already there. The problem for archaeologists is that the extent of this kind of reuse has not always been recognised. Some of the Medieval images have been attributed to the prehistoric period, while others have not been studied systematically because they have rarely been considered of any interest (Martínez García 1995). There is another problem, too. Some of the Christian symbols bear a certain resemblance to those created in prehistory. The two traditions were usually made by different techniques and the later images can also be identified because similar devices occur in dated buildings. Even so, the overlap between these styles is so striking that along the Atlantic coastline a tradition of 'prehistoric' rock art has been recognised which in reality belongs to the Middle Ages (Anati 1968).

But the problem is not always studied in the most informative way. It is of some importance to distinguish between the prehistoric paintings and carvings and the later additions with which they have been confused, yet that approach says very little about the relations between these two groups of images. Were the similarities between them coincidental, or were some of the Christian additions to these sites *intended as interpretations of what was already there*? For example, in the cave at El Pedroso, recently recorded by Lara Alves, there is important evidence for the superimposition of Christian images on prehistoric petroglyphs, the latter most probably dating from the Copper Age or Early Bronze Age (Lara Alves pers. comm.). Here the original carvings included male figures with their arms akimbo. These images had been created with a stone implement, but some of them were selectively recut using a different tool, when only certain features of the original design were emphasised. This had the effect of transforming the depictions of anthropomorphs into drawings of the crucifixion: an interpretation supported by new carvings of crosses elsewhere on the site.

Similar modifications might be made to change other drawings of human figures into pictures of the chalice associated with the Mass, but it may be too simple to assume that this was always done to negate the power of the original design. In some cases it is just as likely that the existing paintings or drawings were *interpreted* in the light of Medieval imagery. Renewing the carvings meant that their significance was also renewed. What were really prehistoric motifs were interpreted as Christian symbols by people who were already accustomed to that visual language. Their mistake was little different from that made by archaeologists. Influenced by their knowledge of ancient art, researchers had misread the Medieval images and had confused them with prehistoric designs.

Romans and the prehistoric past

Rather similar considerations apply to the Roman reception of earlier remains. To add weight to this comparison, the following examples consider the same kinds of archaeological evidence and the same regions of Europe.

One of the most puzzling sites in the study of Iberian rock art is the Roman Iron Age fort of Yecla de Yeltes, in Salamanca (Martín Valls 1983). This is an impressive stone-walled enclosure which is located in the same place as a series of rock outcrops with drawings of abstract motifs and horses. They bear a strong resemblance to the distinctive style of petroglyphs found towards the coastline of North-West Iberia during the third and second millennia BC. The defences at Yecla de Yeltes include a series of stone blocks with further depictions of horses in the same style. The wall face also features a second series of drawings of animals executed in a much cruder technique, most probably using a metal chisel. It is hard to account for all these observations, but it seems possible that the defences were located on a site with an existing series of petroglyphs of Copper Age or Early Bronze Age date. Some of these were removed and employed in the perimeter wall. Copies of these drawings were made in the Roman Iron Age using a different method of stone carving, and these were incorporated in the same construction.

One reason for taking this view is the significance that was obviously attributed to drawings of horses during the Roman period (a suggestion that I owe to Julián Bécares). There is other evidence of this from the Upper Palaeolithic cave of La Griega de Pedraza, in Segovia (Corchón 1997). This site was probably used between about 16,000 and 11,500 BP and contains a series of incised drawings of animals and abstract signs. Nearly 55 per cent of the identifiable animals are horses.

The same cave contains a series of Roman inscriptions, the majority of which are attributed to the Flavian and Severan periods, although the overall sequence extends over a much longer time. The evidence of Roman activity is concentrated in the deepest part of the cave but is generally found in the same places as the Palaeolithic drawings, although the correspondence is not exact (Figure 5.2). The inscriptions are often located next to older depictions of horses.

Although a large number of these inscriptions are personal names and simply record visits to the site, it seems likely that it was a centre of cult activity during

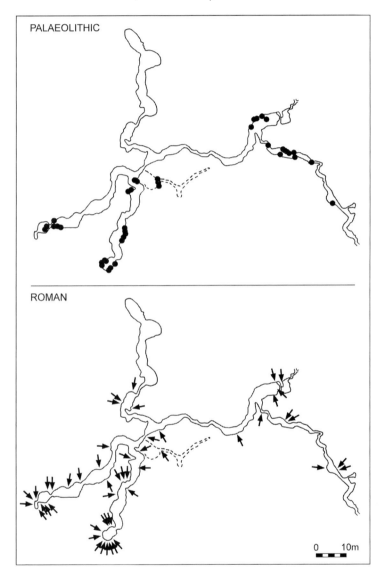

Figure 5.2 Distribution of Palaeolithic images in the cave of La Griega de Pedraza, Northern Spain, in relation to the locations of Roman inscriptions on the same site.

Source: information from Corchón (1997).

this period of reuse. Some of the texts provide hints of its sacred character, and five of them refer to a god and possibly a goddess. There are is also a votive inscription at La Griega, and again this is found among a group of prehistoric engravings of horses.

Such a convergence is unlikely to be coincidental. Not only do the Roman inscriptions in the cave seem to be associated with the Palaeolithic drawings, their positions carefully respect them. Although the evidence is limited by poor survival, these texts also seem to suggest that the cave had a sacred character when it was reused. Since the Palaeolithic carvings would be easy to recognise with the aid of artificial lighting, the link between these two kinds of evidence is likely to be significant. As seems to have happened at Yecla de Yeltes, images from a remote past were imbued with a new significance.

The same argument applies to the Roman reuse of megalithic tombs in Northern France. Again this has been a rather contentious subject, at one time leading to the promulgation of the controversial view that these structures themselves were not Neolithic at all but had actually been built as sacred sites during the Roman period (Collum 1935). In fact the Roman material has a very specialised character. Burials are recorded from the mounds at a number of these monuments (Figure 5.3), while pipe clay figurines are sometimes found near to the entrances of the tombs. Here they occur together with Roman pottery (André 1961; Ars 1997). The main emphasis seems to have been on human fertility, and

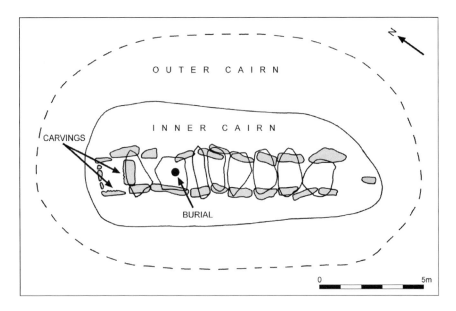

Figure 5.3 The megalithic tomb at Tressé, Northern France, showing the positions of two Neolithic carvings and a Roman burial.

Source: information from Collom (1935).

the figurines usually depict Venus and the Matres. In the case of one site that has already featured in Chapter 2, Le Petit Mont at Arzon, there was also a stone altar which seems to have been intended as a memorial to one of the leading figures in the Roman war against the Veneti (Lecornec 1994). Not all these structures have been particularly well excavated, but a number of them are associated with human remains of this period.

It is obviously difficult to know what the Gallo-Roman population made of these monuments, but there are certain clues. The finds from the reused megaliths in this part of France are of much the same types as those associated with burials and shrines (Galliou 1987: 31 and 151–3). They have little in common with a normal domestic assemblage. Moreover, some of the same kinds of artefacts are associated with striking features of the natural topography, such as caves and rock shelters (ibid.). Like the site of La Griega, these may have been thought of as sacred places during the Roman period. At all events they were quite distinct from other parts of the settled landscape.

The association with Venus and the Matres raises other issues. Allées couvertes can be found with carvings of human breasts which are occasionally linked by a kind of necklace (Shee Twohig 1981: 72–3)). Since some of these images would still have been visible in the Roman period, this may have encouraged the idea that megaliths were specifically female locations. On the other hand, the distribution of these images is rather different from that of the tombs which were reused for burial (Galliou 1987: 31).

Yet another possibility is that by the time that these monuments were reused they could have been confused with another kind of below-ground structure in the same region. These *souterrains* are associated with Iron Age settlements and seem to have gone out of use about 100 BC (Giot 1980; Menez 1994). Most of them are excavated into the solid bedrock and there is only limited evidence of stonework. They are generally interpreted as cellars for the storage of agricultural produce, and yet some of them seem to have contained more specialised deposits. A nineteenth century discovery is particularly relevant to the comparison with megalithic tombs, for in the secondary levels of a souterrain near Quimper there was a large collection of Roman pipe clay figurines (Le Men 1868). It seems possible that, like the Iron Age grain storage pits of North-West Europe, these structures were associated with the fertility of the community and became a focus for offerings when their practical role was over. That may have influenced Roman practice, and the same symbolic system could have extended to the use of Neolithic tombs.

The Middle Ages and the Roman past

We have seen how Medieval Christianity came to terms with the surviving remains of the prehistoric past, and how Roman society accommodated similar kinds of evidence in rather different ways. Still further possibilities arise if we consider how Roman remains were drawn on in the politics of the Middle Ages.

In Chapter 2 I considered origin myths. One of the most powerful myths in the post-Roman period was the descent of the Welsh royal dynasties from Magnus Maximus (Williams 1985: 19–20). He was a Roman general and, for a short time in the late fourth century, the ruler of the Western Empire. Maximus was a native of Spain but had served in Britannia where he fought against the Picts and Scots. He took his army with him to Gaul, where he became Roman emperor in 387. He enjoyed considerable support in Britain, but he never returned there as he died in the following year.

The Welsh connection depends on a mixture of history and legend. Maximus was renamed Macsen Wledig and given a local wife, Helen Luyddog (Helen of the Hosts), who is sometimes identified with St Helena, the mother of the Roman emperor Constantine. Some of the soldiers that Maximus took to Gaul were drawn from the fort of Segontium, close to present day Caernarfon (Caernarvon). Maximus may have introduced foederati from South-East Scotland to protect the local population against Irish raiders, and he is credited with permitting a measure of self government in North Wales.

As Williams says,

> For the purpose of legend at least, this man had the makings of a hero for the Britons. . . . What is remarkable is that he was to become absolutely central to the historical traditions of the Welsh after they entered history hundreds of years later. Gildas, a west Briton writing in the sixth century, dated the fall of Roman Britain from the 'withdrawal of the legions' by Maximus. Welsh tradition was to assert that Maximus had done something wonderful for the Welsh people. . . . The early poetry and traditions of the Welsh are . . . suffused with memories of Maximus. . . . Nearly every dynasty which was to claw its way to power in Wales took pains to construct genealogies which linked their names with that of Maximus.
>
> (1985: 20)

If the Welsh traced their history back to a Roman emperor, their enemies could take a similar course. Late in the thirteenth century the English king, Edward I, was to appropriate exactly the same legend. Caernarvon Castle was a symbol of his victory over the Welsh and was located in a position that was both strategically and historically important (Taylor 1986: 77–103). It replaced a Norman motte, but it was also close to the ruins of the Roman fort of Segontium, from which Maximus had taken his soldiers to Gaul. Such was the importance of Segontium that in the twelfth century it had been described as the city of the emperor Constantine.

Edward used the same associations to emphasise his sovereignty over the Welsh. In 1283, the body of Magnus Maximus was discovered, most probably in the ruins of Segontium, and was given Christian burial on Edward's instructions. That was the year in which the Welsh were finally defeated, and it was also when a great castle was built to consolidate English authority.

This was a castle unlike any other. In the collection of tales known as the *Mabinogion*, Macsen Wledig dreams of returning to Wales and building a city and a great fort *with towers of many colours*. Edward fulfilled that dream. Caernarvon was an English castle but was in a completely unfamiliar style:

> The difference consists chiefly in the choice of polygonal instead of the more usual round towers or turrets, and in the prominent patterning of the walls with bands of differently coloured stone. For the former there were few, and for the latter no English precedents. Banded masonry was not uncommon in medieval Italian architecture, but for its use in conjunction with polygonal towers there was one celebrated precedent: the tile-laced Theodosian walls of Constantinople, the first Constantine's own city. The resemblance seems too striking to be fortuitous. . . . It would seem that the new building was intended from the outset to recall Caernarvon's legendary past and to exemplify it in the architectural forms of the imperial power with which that past was associated.
>
> (Taylor 1986: 78–9)

The chain of connections is entirely plausible. The appearance of the new castle matches the description of Magnus Maximus's capital in the *Mabinogion*, but it was an English king who built it. The legendary link between Segontium and Constantine is emphasised by building in the same architectural style as the defences of Constantinople, and the mortal remains of Maximus himself were discovered and reburied on Edward's instructions in the very same year as the Welsh were defeated and work began on the castle.

In South Wales, the Roman inheritance was seen in a very different light. Here our concern is with the legionary fortress at Caerleon. Parts of the Roman fabric were clearly apparent in the early Middle Ages, in particular the remains of the baths, and a triumphal arch that was located at the centre of the site. Not surprisingly, these massive masonry structures attracted interest and interpretation, but in this case they became associated, not with the Roman empire, but with King Arthur. Giraldus Cambrensis described a great tower at Caerleon when he visited the ruins, but it was Geoffrey of Monmouth's *History of the Kings of Britain* that really popularised the Arthurian legend and emphasised its connection with the site.

That happened in the early twelfth century and seems to have accompanied a resurgence of Welsh opposition to the influence of the English crown. The political history of the period is a complicated one, with many changes in local allegiances and in the fortunes of the lords of Caerleon, but it seems to reach a climax in the early to mid thirteenth century with the demolition of both the buildings that had taken on so much significance.

This was an enormous task, as the baths and the triumphal arch were considerable structures and seem to have been well preserved. Their removal required a large labour force and careful co-ordination, and yet there is little evidence that they provided a particularly useful source of material for new building projects. Suitable stone could have been obtained from other parts of Caerleon with much less effort. The demolition of these buildings may have been a symbolic act and has been characterised by Howell as 'the deliberate erasure of memory' (2000: 394). He summarises the argument in these terms:

> A body of literature placed Caerleon at the forefront of kingship in Wales. Here was a site with imposing architecture which was presented as no less than the court of Arthur. . . . For the marcher barons, physical remains which were associated in the native mind with Welsh authority and kingship would be undesirable. . . . The possibility of expunging the physical evidence of Welsh lordship, which the Roman remains seem to have become, would have been sufficient to provide the spur. . . . The purpose of the demolition gangs was more than levelling buildings; their remit may also have been to remove physical symbols of an . . . earlier Welsh tradition.
>
> (ibid.: 394)

This is the exact opposite of the situation at Caernarvon where a Roman architectural model was used to enforce English power and was assimilated to a local origin myth. At Caerleon, on the other hand, Roman remains were interpreted in terms of Welsh resistance to the English, and in this case had to be removed.

Summary: the reasons for reuse

There will have been many places where such connections elude archaeological analysis – sites with particularly auspicious associations, sites at which particular events had happened, those associated with supernatural beings – and these will only be identified through the study of folklore and place names. But for all the instances in which such connections remain unexplained, there will be others that conform to more general models. That is true of all the cases quoted here.

These examples have covered a considerable period of time and have involved the archaeology of several countries, from Italy to Wales. What they have in common is that something is known about the reasons why ancient sites were reused. In some instances this is because information exists on the relationship of Christian communities to the remains of a pagan past. The same applies to the Roman period, too. There is historical evidence for the distinctive nature of Roman religion, and in one of the cases quoted here, the cave of La Griega, there is a series of inscriptions which can still be understood. The Welsh examples are different again, for while they do draw on literary sources, that has more to do with the promulgation of origin myths than it does with modern notions of history. In every case there is good reason to suggest why ancient sites assumed a new significance.

The title of this section suggests some possibilities. It refers to *interpretation*, *confrontation* and *legitimation*, and each of these can be illustrated by the examples considered so far.

Interpretation is perhaps the most difficult concept of the three, because the case depends on particularly elusive evidence. In this chapter I have suggested several instances in which this approach may be helpful. The anthropomorphic paintings and carvings of Copper Age and Bronze Age Iberia may have been interpreted through their modification during the Christian era. In some cases the original signs were left intact when Medieval motifs were created on the same surfaces, but in other instances the two groups of images were superimposed or combined. That enhanced the existing resemblance between these motifs and effected the transformation of human figures from a pagan past into drawings of chalices and the crucifixion. This may only have been possible because the older symbols were already understood as Christian imagery. In the same way, the Gallo-Roman people who reused Breton megaliths may not have known that these dated from the remote past. The offerings that they made there are very like those found at shrines, and these half-buried structures may well have been viewed in the same light as the caves and rock shelters where similar material was deposited. The same could also apply to the ritual significance of souterrains, and it is by no means certain that people in the past were able to distinguish between these different structures in the ways that archaeologists do now. That is equally true of sacred caves in Spain. There is no reason to suppose that the Romans who visited them would have been aware that the drawings of horses on the walls at La Griega were any older than the those at Yecla de Yeltes. Clearly, horses played an important part in local belief, so what could be more natural than to assimilate these ancient drawings to those that were newly made? To think otherwise would assume a modern understanding of chronology.

We know from the history of the church that the remains of the pagan past could either be assimilated into the fabric of the new religion or they could be destroyed. That is obvious from the examples considered here. There are cases in which the ruins of megalithic tombs were incorporated within ecclesiastical buildings, and other instances in which a standing stone, associated with pagan worship, was changed into a Christian cross. Chambered tombs could be converted into churches, or Christian cemeteries could develop alongside. I quoted two detailed examples of this practice in Normandy and the contrast between them is revealing. In one case the distribution of the graves was towards the entrance of the prehistoric tomb, but in the other example a similar monument was destroyed and replaced by a church. Such a development could have happened much more widely, and in early Medieval Wales the Roman remains associated with King Arthur were levelled to the ground when they became too closely associated with opposition to English authority.

The last example also came from Wales and represents the most sophisticated interpretation of all. This is where two different groups of people tried to exploit the same origin myth for political ends and did so through the use of material culture. For the Welsh dynasties, the ruins of Segontium were the visible proof of their descent from Magnus Maximus. He was buried there and the surviving fabric was what remained of the city of his son, the emperor Constantine. For Edward I, on the other hand, the body of Maximus was a relic which came under his control at the time of the Welsh defeat, and the building of Caernarvon Castle was the fulfilment of the emperor's plan recorded in the *Mabinogion*. Edward's appropriation of Welsh tradition is made more obvious by the design of the castle itself, for its exotic features can be interpreted as a reference to the city of Constantinople. Its construction was not only a response to the legendary history of the Welsh, it was also an attempt to legitimise their conquest through an appeal to tradition.

SCALES OF ANALYSIS

Introduction

The examples considered so far illustrate particular kinds of relationship between the present and the past and identify some of the principles behind the reuse of antiquity. It remains to explore the different scales at which such evidence can be studied. The second part of this chapter begins by considering the pattern of reuse over a long period and an extensive area. It is concerned with the ways in which different kinds of prehistoric burial places in Northern Germany were treated in subsequent periods. We then consider the relationship of just one type of prehistoric monument – an Iron Age enclosure – to the history of the locations in which it was built. We do so by comparing rather similar evidence from France, Belgium and the Netherlands with that from Lowland Britain. Finally, the discussion focuses on the development of just one major site: the group of prehistoric and early Medieval monuments which make up the royal complex at Tara, in Ireland. Each scale of analysis has different insights to impart.

Regional patterning: the reuse of mortuary sites in North Germany

How far can the reuse of antiquities be investigated at a regional scale? There have been few studies of this kind, but, curiously enough, two of them are concerned with the same part of Europe. For that reason the differences between their results are particularly revealing.

One of these studies, by Holtorf, appeared in 1998, while the other, by Sopp, came out in the following year. Holtorf's analysis has a more restricted geographical and chronological range as it is concerned with the later history of the megalithic tombs of Mecklenburg-Vorpommern, in North-East Germany. Sopp's monograph covers a larger area and a longer period of time. He discusses the reuse of three kinds of field monument – megaliths, round barrows and flat graves – over a large area of North Germany, extending from the River Oder to the east as far as the Rhine to the west. His study also extends southwards to Dresden and Cologne.

The two analyses belong to very different traditions. Holtorf (1998) locates his research within the framework of post-processual archaeology and offers a 'biographical' approach to the history of megalithic tombs between their creation in the Neolithic period and AD 1400. Sopp (1999) follows a more traditional method. He makes no reference to theoretical writings and never mentions Holtorf's earlier work in the same field. His analysis is detailed and well documented, but he offers little explanation of the patterns that he finds; their identification seems to be sufficient in itself. Like Holtorf, Sopp begins his study with the building of megalithic tombs and ends it in the Middle Ages, in this case at AD 1300 (Table 5.1).

The value of using both these studies is that it allows us to ask a number of questions that could not be answered by reading either of them in isolation. How widely distributed are the patterns of monument reuse identified by Holtorf and by Sopp? Are they found throughout North Germany, or do they provide evidence of more local traditions? Were all these monuments accorded the same treatment during later periods, or did the original forms of these sites mean that they went through different kinds of histories? These questions can be addressed by comparing the two accounts.

The first question is the easiest to answer. It is clear that the pattern of reuse identified by Holtorf does not characterise the region as a whole. The megaliths in his study area often developed throughout the Neolithic period and remained important in the Early Bronze Age, when many of the monuments were closed. After that, the main phases in which these tombs were brought back into use seem to have been the Late Bronze Age, the Early Iron Age and the Migration period. These patterns do not extend across the entire area studied by Sopp, for in this case there was less activity in post-Roman times.

The same point is evident from the distribution maps published by Sopp. Prehistoric monuments with evidence of later reuse are widely distributed, but at

Table 5.1 The frequency of reuse of Neolithic or Early Bronze Age mortuary sites in Northern Germany by total number of examples considered

	Structural link to original monument (%)	Renewed activity nearby (%)
Late Bronze Age/Early Iron Age	17	14
Pre-Roman Iron Age	39	6
Roman period	18	34
Migration period	8	7
Early Medieval	11	19
Medieval	7	20

Source: information from Sopp (1999).

certain times this activity seems to have focused on specific areas. In the Late Bronze Age/Early Iron Age it is a particular feature of the region around Leipzig, and in the following phase it is equally strongly represented between Hamburg and Berlin (Figure 5.4).

It is also evident that people in the past were able to distinguish between the two main classes of monument studied by Sopp. They must have thought that the differences were important as they reused these sites in separate periods. Thus the principal phases in which megaliths were reused were the Late Bronze Age and the Pre-Roman Iron Age. Again there was activity on the sites of round barrows in the Pre-Roman Iron Age, but in this case it continued into the Roman period. The histories of these monuments show a certain overlap but it seems as if some of the burial mounds assumed a new importance as the significance of megaliths declined. Flat graves show yet another pattern, with two main periods of reuse, in the Roman Iron Age and the early Middle Ages. This is especially interesting as the positions of these graves must have been marked. Their locations were remembered when they were not in use.

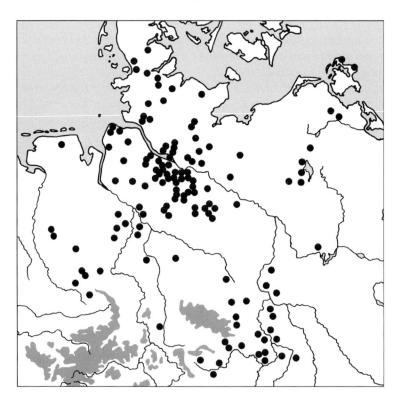

Figure 5.4 The distribution of earlier burial monuments in North Germany reused during the Pre-Roman Iron Age.

Source: information from Sopp (1999).

So far this analysis has looked for very general patterning in the history of particular kinds of site and has attempted to identify the main periods of reuse. There is a disadvantage in this kind of study, for it tends to overlook the very complex sequences observed at individual monuments, where a particular structure might be renewed not once but several times. That is the strength of the biographical approach favoured by Holtorf, although his own case studies are limited to developments at megalithic tombs.

I shall illustrate this point with some specific examples, each of them related to one of the types of mortuary monument investigated by Sopp. As we have seen, in his study area the megalithic tombs showed the simplest pattern of reuse, with a major emphasis on the Late Bronze Age and Pre-Roman Iron Age. A typical example of this is Barendorf where a small stone cist was built inside an existing megalith and was associated with a series of Late Bronze Age urns and a single find of metalwork (Sopp 1999: 180–1). Similar evidence comes from other chambered tombs, yet monuments of this kind could be treated in much the same way during later phases. For the most part, renewed activity at these sites seems to have been confined to a single period. In Holtorf's study area the sequence was rather more complex, but this is partly because he was able to draw on the results of quite recent excavations. Although most of the secondary burials belonged to the periods mentioned earlier, inside these monuments there were artefacts dating from other phases.

This is quite different from the sequence observed at round barrows. One of Sopp's sites is especially famous. This is the well known barrow at Leubingen, which covered a mortuary house associated with a rich burial dating from about 1900 BC (Figure 5.5). This was covered by a cairn and buried beneath a considerable mound (ibid.: 238–9). What is less well known is that the barrow was reused as the site of a Medieval cemetery. No fewer than seventy inhumations were found in the top of the mound, laid out east–west and associated with rings, ornaments and knives.

This is perhaps an extreme case, for more of the barrows in Northern

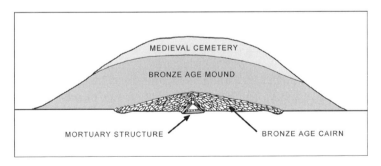

Figure 5.5 Schematic cross-section of the multi-period burial mound at Leubingen, North Germany.

Source: information from Sopp (1999).

Germany were reused during later prehistory. One of Sopp's most convincing examples is at Kalbsrieth where a sequence of burials beneath a major round barrow began in the Corded Ware phase (ibid.: 228–9). The site retained its importance in the Baalberge Culture, then the Globular Amphora Culture and the Unétice Culture. The monument was reused in the La Tène Iron Age, again in the Migration period and finally it became an early Medieval cemetery. During that time there is evidence that the original mound was enlarged on at least two occasions, the first during the Corded Ware phase and the second during the currency of Globular Amphorae. Although there were some periods in which the site was not used for burial, the sequence starts with a Neolithic grave and ends in the Middle Ages with the addition of a cemetery.

Not all the sequences are as complex as this, but it is quite common for the use of an individual site to extend over more than one phase, with no clear evidence of activity in between them. Thus, at Oeversee, Roman Iron Age burials were inserted into a barrow that had been built in the Early Bronze Age (Bauch *et al.* 1989: Abb 13), and at Quedlingburg a Late Neolithic round barrow was reused in two quite different periods, first for cremation burials in the La Tène Iron Age and then for an inhumation cemetery of early Medieval date (Sopp 1999: 267–8) (Figure 5.6).

Such evidence suggests two observations. First, it seems likely that round barrows were reused on more occasions than megaliths, even when some of those mounds originated in the Neolithic period. Second, there is little to suggest the continuous use of a long-lived monument, for the sequences observed at individual sites often seem to be broken by intervals in which there is no evidence of activity. It may be that some of the round barrows remained important for a longer time than the megalithic tombs.

The flat cemeteries raise different problems. In many cases they are found outside, or in between, the remains of existing monuments, suggesting that their positions were established by reference to these structures. There is no consistent relationship between the date of the original site and that of the graves that developed around it. For example, a megalithic tomb at Gudendorf is accompanied by a flat cemetery of the Late Roman and Migration periods (Tempel 1981). Similarly, one Neolithic round barrow at Herne-Schloss is accompanied by burials of Early Bronze Age and Roman dates, and another at Unterstedt by deposits of Migration period and early Medieval origin (Sopp 1999: 221–3 and 293–4). Similarly, the Bronze Age barrows are accompanied on one site by an Iron Age flat cemetery, and on another by Roman Iron Age burials. Further examples of activity close to Bronze Age burial mounds include the development of cemeteries during the Late Roman, Migration and early Medieval periods. There is no sign of a single pattern.

There are also flat cemeteries which exist in their own right, although they may have formed in two or more phases, separated by an interval. In this case it seems likely that the positions of the first group of burials had been remembered or marked. For example, at Cörmigk later burials respect the positions of no

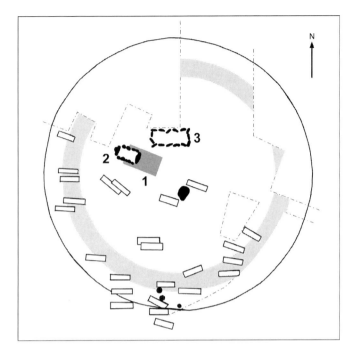

Figure 5.6 Diagram summarising the sequence of burials at Quedlingburg, North Germany.

Source: information from Sopp (1999).

Key
1: the primary Late Neolithic grave; 2 and 3: secondary Late Neolithic burials; ●: Iron Age cremations; ⬜: early Medieval graves.

fewer than six Late Neolithic or Early Bronze Age graves, which do not seem to have been accompanied by any monument (Laser 1959). It is not clear how their position was known.

Such flat graves pose many problems. They show less sign of a punctuated sequence of reuse than the round barrows, and yet this sometimes occurs. In that case, the positions of the older graves may well have been known, for few of them were disturbed during later periods. That is less of an issue where these cemeteries were established next to existing monuments, but even then there does not seem to be any consistent relationship between the age of the original structure and the period or periods in which these cemeteries were established.

To sum up, these studies suggest that people had made quite specific choices over the kinds of monuments they reused: choices that mean that they must have been well aware of the distinction between round barrows and megaliths. They could also recall the positions of flat cemeteries, even after lengthy periods in which those sites were deserted. What is less clear is quite why such choices were made. It may only be possible to address that question by working on a more local scale. There is already some evidence that different communities expressed different attitudes to the past, so that the broad tendencies identified in this account were subject to regional variation. That provides one starting point for another kind of enquiry.

Patterning by monument type: the reception of La Tène funerary enclosures in Continental Europe

There are other regions in which there do seem to have been connections between different monuments on the same site, even if their construction and use were separated by a significant period of time.

Here the story moves to Northern France. One of the best known categories of Iron Age monuments are the square barrows and mortuary enclosures of the Marne Champagne region. They have achieved this reputation because so many of them contain elaborate graves which include weapons, personal ornaments and finds of dismantled vehicles (Demoule 1999). But the tradition to which these monuments are linked has a more general currency in the La Tène period. On the broadest level, it may also extend to the remains of earthwork shrines and to the small wooden buildings found inside them. Nor are all these enclosures confined to the north of France, for it is clear that other examples can be identified in Belgium and the Netherlands (Wilhelmi 1990). It is even possible that the distinctive Viereckschanzen of Central Europe conform to the same archetype, but it is by no means obvious that they are a unitary class of monument, or that all these sites played a specialised role (Büchsenschütz, Olivier and Aillières 1989; Bittel 1998).

What is apparent is that the use of small square enclosures in cemeteries emerged in the early La Tène period. These earthworks co-existed with a variety of circular monuments of entirely local types, although in some cases they replaced them over time. It seems likely that this happened in response to developments in religious belief that originated outside those regions. Despite the similarities between the square enclosures in different parts of Continental Europe, there is little uniformity in the burial rite, and the exceptionally rich graves known in Northern France are only one manifestation of this wider development.

Because the adoption of square enclosures and barrows seems to conform to a specific chronological horizon it is all too easy to overlook their local context. Many of the new enclosures emerge during the development of well established cemeteries, and in these instances there is no sign of a sudden break in the sequence. In other cases, however, the new types of enclosure are more closely connected with older monuments. The following examples illustrate the principal relationships.

Most of the evidence concerns the relations of square enclosures to round barrows, but there are occasional links between these monuments, settlements and megaliths. One of the sites mentioned earlier, Portejoie in Normandy, not only illustrates the connection between an allée couverte and a series of Christian graves, it is also linked directly to an Iron Age enclosure of this kind. It dated from the first century BC and contained over thirty burials (Carré 1993) (Figure 5.7). The earthwork ran up to the end wall of the chambered tomb and was associated with a small ring ditch. There seems little doubt that these relationships were as carefully contrived as those between the Neolithic monument and the Christian burials.

At Conchil-le-Temple, Pas de Calais, we can observe an equally striking connection between a settlement site and a group of Bronze Age barrows (Pinnigre 1990) (Figure 5.8). In this case, fieldwork has identified a row of large circular mounds, two of which had coalesced during the development of the cemetery. They were the largest monuments in the excavated area. During the La Tène Iron Age, the site was occupied by a settlement, defined by a square enclosure whose ditch encapsulated the positions of the principal mounds and

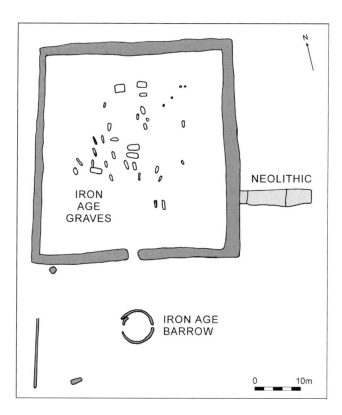

Figure 5.7 Neolithic collective tomb at Portjoie, Northern France, reused as an Iron Age cemetery.

Source: information from Carré (1993).

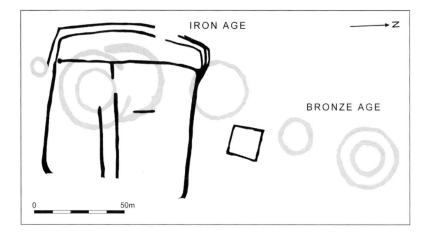

Figure 5.8 The Bronze Age barrow cemetery at Conchil-le-Temple, Northern France, overlain by a series of Iron Age enclosures. The larger square enclosure contains a settlement, while the small square earthwork to its north is interpreted as a ritual monument.

Source: information from Pinnigre (1990).

skirted the remains of two others. This enclosure contained a series of domestic buildings. Outside the settlement a small square earthwork was built in between two of the Bronze Age barrows. This also dated from the middle of the Iron Age. It was exactly like the monuments that were used for burial at that time. The site had been transformed: the principal burial mounds were incorporated in the heart of the settled area and a new ritual focus developed nearby.

Where the square enclosures did not develop into cemeteries of the same date, they were sometimes linked to the positions of older barrows. This is quite widely documented, although their relationship takes several different forms. On some sites it involves changes to the layout of the cemetery as a whole, while in other cases there is more evidence for the transformation of individual mounds.

For example, at Soucy in the valley of the Yonne a cemetery of at least twenty round barrows was established during the Late Bronze Age (Baray *et al.* 1994). Only one grave was dug during the following phase, Hallstatt C, and in Hallstatt D just two of the existing round barrows were reused. A hiatus followed in the early La Tène period and then, during a final phase, the remains of the largest barrow on the site were flanked by no fewer than seven square or rectangular enclosures (Figure 5.9). There was a break in the development of the cemetery but, compared with the sequences traced by Holtorf and by Sopp, it was of short duration. On the other hand, like many sites in North Germany, Soucy was reused as a cemetery in the Middle Ages.

At other sites that relationship between Bronze Age and La Tène earthworks takes a more explicit form. Two examples are particularly revealing. At Ursel-

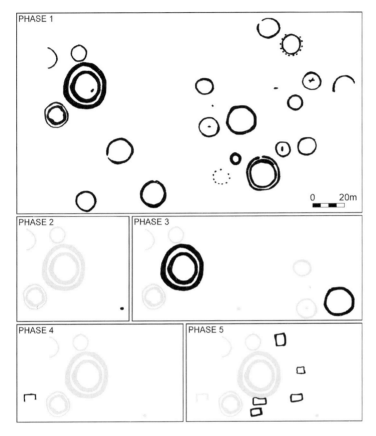

Figure 5.9 The archaeological sequence in the cemetery at Soucy, Northern France.
The prehistoric use of the site extends from Bronze Final IIIb (Phase 1)
to La Tène B2 (Phase 5).

Source: information from Baray *et al.* (1994).

Rosenstraat in Belgium, a round barrow had been built in the Early or Middle
Bronze Age and was reconstructed in the following phase (Bourgeois 1998).
Then it was left intact. In the Late Iron Age, this structure was renewed and the
existing earthwork was defined by a square enclosure which respected one
segment of the original barrow ditch. A small cemetery was established on the
site and continued to be important in the Roman period. Thus a circular mound
that developed during the Bronze Age was rebuilt in a more appropriate form
when the monument was reused.

Something rather similar happened at La Calotterie in Picardy, where two
round barrows of Bronze Age date have been excavated (Desfossées 1998)
(Figure 5.10). The remains of one of these earthworks was left intact during
the Iron Age, but towards the end of that period a small square earthwork

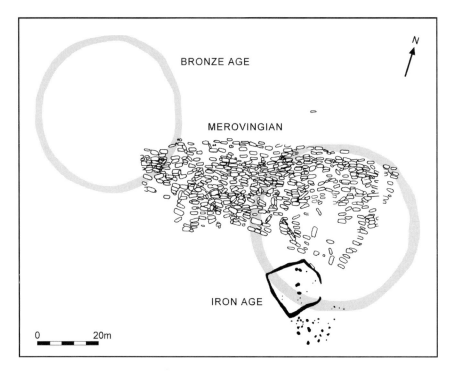

Figure 5.10 Bronze Age barrows at La Calotterie, Northern France, overlain by an Iron Age enclosure accompanied by a small cemetery. The site was reused by Merovingian graves.

Source: information from Desfossées (1998).

was established on the flank of the other mound. This overlay the original barrow ditch and was associated with two main groups of burials, one of them within the enclosure and the other just outside it. As so often, the sequence did not end there, and a massive Merovingian cemetery was established on the same site. This extended between the two Bronze Age round barrows, but respected the remains of one of the mounds and the position of the Late Iron Age burials.

These different relationships take a very distinctive form. Some of the La Tène enclosures were associated with round barrows. On many sites they were added to existing cemeteries, but, where this did not happen, there would have been little problem in linking them with the remains of older mounds. That was because monuments of this kind were still being built. Indeed, Middle and Late Iron Age enclosures were often connected with barrows that had been used in the Late Bronze Age, or even during Hallstatt C. Their significance could still have been remembered, in which case the hiatus in the use of the cemetery may not have presented the problems that it would have done under other circumstances.

The reception of La Tène enclosures in Lowland England

There is another region in which a tradition of small square or rectangular enclosures became established in the Iron Age. This is Lowland Britain, but here the evidence presents particular problems. The tradition of building square barrows is well known in East Yorkshire, where it is associated with a series of unusually rich burials of the type found on the Continent (Stead 1991). Elsewhere, these monuments are difficult to characterise and still more difficult to date. Some of them may have been free-standing enclosures rather than mounds, and individual examples may represent the remains of small timber buildings. Few are associated with graves. Moreover, such structures have a lengthy history in the British Isles. The earliest do seem to date from the Iron Age, but similar features can be found on Roman sites and may even be associated with early Medieval cemeteries. Blair (1995) has argued that earthworks of this kind form a long-running tradition of pagan shrines.

Despite the close resemblance between these monuments and Iron Age earthworks in Continental Europe, there is a difference in the ways in which they were used. As we have seen, the Continental examples are often found on the sites of existing cemeteries, where the square enclosures and barrows supplement, and possibly replace, an existing tradition of round mounds. Where these sites had a discontinuous history, the same association between different kinds of monument seems to have been important and Iron Age structures were closely linked to those that had existed a few centuries before. The hiatus was short enough for something of the significance of these earlier sites to have been remembered.

This could not have been the case in Britain, where the building of round barrows declined rapidly after the Early Bronze Age. That means that when elements of the new ideology were adopted in Lowland England any direct connection with these older monuments had been lost. In fact, in East Yorkshire, the one region with a well established tradition of square barrows, Iron Age burial mounds are often in different places from those of Bronze Age date (Stoertz 1987).

Here we should recall Barrett's account of the mythological landscape of Iron Age Britain, quoted in Chapter 1 (Barrett 1999). He made the point that the burial mounds of earlier prehistory would have played a vital part in the experience of later communities, even when those sites were no longer used. They occupied such a conspicuous place in the landscape that people had to include them in their understanding of the world. Even by leaving them untouched they were acknowledging their importance.

Barrett was writing about Southern Britain, and his argument was undoubtedly influenced by the large amount of fieldwork that has been conducted in Wessex. His paper is an admirable account of the evidence from that particular area and might apply just as convincingly to the archaeology of the Yorkshire Wolds, but it is not consistent with the evidence from other regions, for here there is an increasing body of information to show that Iron Age communities could also appropriate the remains of older sites. The role of small square enclosures is of particular importance here. If Continental monuments of this kind only occasionally acknowledged the traces of the past, in England this seems to have been a regular occurrence.

There are very few cases in which late prehistoric settlements were directly superimposed on the remains of Bronze Age burial mounds, nor are there many examples of Iron Age monuments associated with long barrows and related structures. One is on the Yorkshire Wolds at Kirkburn, where a square enclosure overlay a ditched monument of Neolithic date (Stead 1991: 24–8). At Uley in Gloucestershire, an Iron Age enclosure was tacked on to the end of a rather similar structure. In this case it was associated with a number of distinctive deposits of human remains, spearheads, personal ornaments and Late Iron Age coins. The site developed into a major temple during the Roman period (Woodward and Leach 1993).

Another important site is at Maxey in Cambridgeshire (Pryor *et al.* 1985: chapters 2 and 3) (Figure 5.11). This includes several elements of Neolithic date, but one monument seems to have been particularly important at that time. This was an oval barrow, which was located in the path of a cursus. Two square

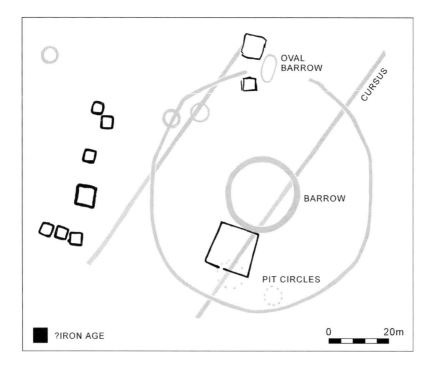

Figure 5.11 Earlier prehistoric monuments, including a cursus, an oval mound, pit circles and round barrows at Maxey, Eastern England, associated with a series of Iron Age square enclosures.

Source: information from Pryor *et al.* (1985).

enclosures of Iron Age date were built immediately alongside the mound, both of them sharing the same alignment as that monument. The mound itself was incorporated in the entrance of a large circular earthwork, most probably a henge, with a round barrow at its centre. Another seven square enclosures were situated just outside the henge, while a larger earthwork of similar outline was constructed in the interior. It seems as if every component of the Neolithic complex was accompanied by monuments of Iron Age date.

More of these small square enclosures are juxtaposed with the remains of Bronze Age burial mounds. For instance, at Holt in Worcestershire part of a Bronze Age barrow cemetery was incorporated inside another rectilinear earthwork (Hunt, Shotliff and Woodhouse 1986). This respected the position of one of the round barrows and cut another in half, but there is no evidence of any houses on this site. Instead, a small square structure, possibly the remains of a wooden building, is located in the centre of the monument. Beside it is a structure of exactly the same form, which was erected over part of an earlier round barrow. The placing of these different features seem to have been deliberately planned.

A more complex sequence has been identified at Caistor St Edmund in Norfolk (Ashwin and Bates 2000: chapter 4) (Figure 5.12). There were at least four Bronze Age round barrows on this site, as well as a circular earthwork enclosing a ring of posts. These were supplemented by three smaller mounds in the Later Bronze Age, when the position of the existing cemetery was incorporated within a settlement. The Late Iron Age saw a complete change in the way in which the area was used. Five square or rectangular structures were built during this phase, and these were arranged in a line leading from the site of the timber circle to a large round barrow on the edge of the cemetery. The nature of these constructions is not always clear, but one of them was almost certainly a wooden building very similar to the shrines that have been discovered inside hillforts of the same period. Close to it there was an Iron Age cremation.

This particular structure had been built inside an earthwork enclosure dating from the Early Bronze Age. It also overlay part of the timber circle associated with that monument. Another square enclosure abutted the position of a Later Bronze Age house, whose location might still have been remembered, and the entire range of Iron Age structures was orientated on another component of the original barrow cemetery. But the development of the site did not end during the Iron Age, for just beyond either end of this alignment of square enclosures there were Anglo-Saxon graves. The reuse of these particular monuments extended beyond the prehistoric period.

A similar development may have taken place at Westhampnett in Sussex, where a cemetery dating from the earlier first century BC has been excavated (Fitzpatrick 1997) (Figure 5.13). This contained a large number of burials and a series of cremation pyres, but towards the edge of this complex there was also a series of square or rectangular structures which are interpreted as shrines. These were located to the east of the Iron Age burials close to the positions of two ploughed round barrows. Unfortunately, the barrows themselves lacked any

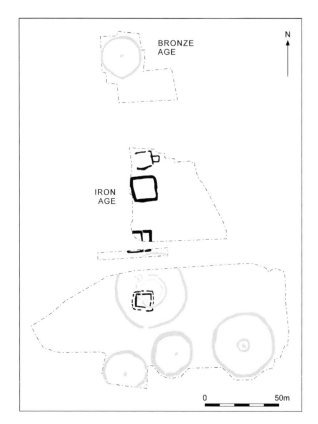

Figure 5.12 Early Bronze Age monuments at Caistor St Edmund, Eastern England,
        associated with a series of Iron Age square enclosures and a wooden shrine.

Source: information from Ashwin and Bates (2000).

dating evidence and the sequence is made more complicated by the presence of
further burials on the site during the Roman and Anglo-Saxon periods. On the
other hand, a third round barrow, only 300 metres away, dates from the early
Bronze Age. Beside it there was a Roman site which may also have been a shrine.
In its original form this was another square enclosure. It was eventually
reconstructed on a larger scale and may have had an eastern entrance facing the
older mound (see Figure 5.13; I am grateful to Andrew Fitzpatrick for allowing
me to make use of this material in advance of publication).

The evidence from Westhampnett is similar to that from Caistor St Edmund,
and in each case it is possible that a series of Iron Age shrines was constructed in
relation to the positions of Bronze Age round barrows. At Westhampnett that
must remain a hypothesis, but it is certainly what seems to have happened on
a neighbouring site during the second century AD. Like Caistor St Edmund,
Westhampnett included some Anglo-Saxon graves, and three of these were also

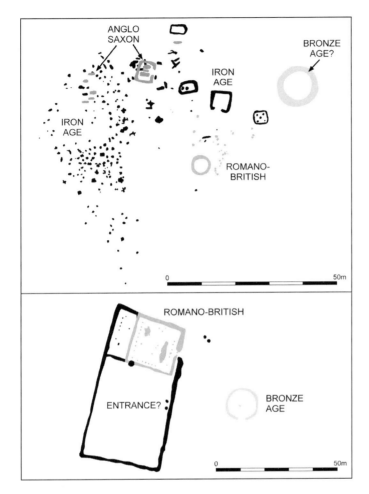

Figure 5.13 (*Upper*) Iron Age, Roman and Anglo-Saxon enclosures and associated burials, juxtaposed with round barrows or ring ditches at Westhampnett, Southern England. (*Lower*) A second site nearby where a Roman enclosure, interpreted as a possible shrine, is orientated on a Bronze Age round barrow.

Source: information courtesy of Andrew Fitzpatrick.

within a square enclosure, adding weight to the idea that this was a long-lived form of funerary architecture (Blair 1995). The Iron Age cremation cemetery raises yet another possibility as the excavator has pointed out that the burials were grouped around a circular space which remained largely free of features. This has about the same diameter – 13 metres – as the Bronze Age round barrow nearby. Is it possible that the Iron Age burials respected the position of an earthen mound that has since been removed by the plough?

Sites like these represent the most common relationship between Bronze Age round barrows and what are regarded as late prehistoric shrines. As we have seen, similar associations continued to be formed during the Roman period. But there are two other sites that deserve to be considered here, for they provide evidence of a different way of reusing an older mound. One is at Grendon in Northamptonshire and the other at Willington in Bedfordshire (Jackson 1995; Dawson 1996) (Figure 5.14). In each case a Bronze Age barrow was incorporated into an Iron Age enclosure, but these are not the small square monuments that have been considered so far. They are elongated monuments more like some of the ceremonial sites of the Neolithic period. At Grendon, a trapezoidal enclosure

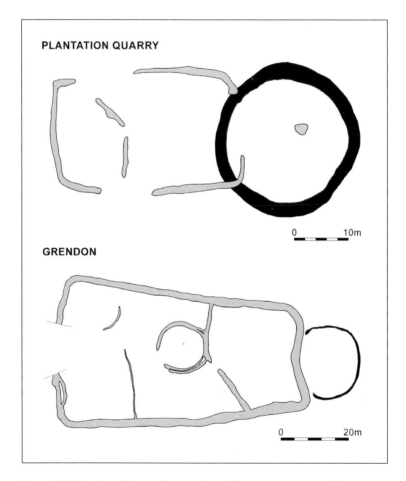

Figure 5.14 Two Iron Age enclosures (tinted) incorporating older Bronze Age round barrows at Plantation Quarry, Willington, and Grendon in the English Midlands.

Source: information from Jackson (1995) and Dawson (1996).

runs up to the position of an existing burial mound but leaves its structure intact. Within this enclosure was a circular building; although this has been interpreted as a house, it may have played a more specialised role. Much the same happened at Willington. The two sites have a number of features in common: they are of roughly the same proportions, both include at least one internal subdivision, and each site follows an east–west alignment with a Bronze Age round barrow at one end. At Willington, the relationship between these features is particularly obvious as the enclosure extends into the edge of the mound. Moreover, an Iron Age pit, containing pig bones, was dug at the centre of the barrow and was located on the long axis of the monument.

Why were such relationships so important, and why were there certain contrasts between the settings of these late prehistoric sites on either side of the Channel? The adoption of square enclosures and barrows may have taken place at about the same time in Britain and Continental Europe and could reflect the adoption of new religious ideas in the La Tène period. In France, Belgium and the Netherlands these influenced the organisation of well established cemeteries, many of which had been in use since the Bronze Age. New concepts could be assimilated and take on the authority of the past. Only occasionally was it necessary to create that link with antiquity by connecting the new generation of monuments to sites that were no longer in use. Even when it happened, the existing structures had been built so recently that something might still have been known of their original associations.

That would not have been possible in England, where more of the enclosures and mounds were directly linked to monuments surviving from the past. That was not true on the Yorkshire Wolds, but in other areas the main links that were forged during the Iron Age were with earthworks of Early Bronze Age or even Neolithic date. That is hardly surprising as the tradition of building burial mounds was virtually over by 1000 BC. Where it was easy to incorporate the new kinds of monument into existing cemeteries on the Continent, that would not have been possible in Britain, and it may explain why the small square enclosures of the Iron Age are so often associated with the remains of much earlier constructions. Far from being left alone, as Barrett suggests, some of the Bronze Age barrows were brought back into commission and provided a certain legitimacy for new ways of celebrating the dead and the supernatural.

Monument reuse at a single site: the archaeology of Tara

That discussion was limited to relations between England and parts of Continental Europe. It would not describe the situation in prehistoric Ireland. That is because there is evidence that round barrows were built there from the Neolithic period through to the Iron Age (Raftery 1994: chapter 4). Moreover, it seems as if large circular enclosures allied to henges may have been important over the same period of time. These features are found together at the Irish 'royal sites'

(Wailes 1982; Raftery 1994: chapter 8), and it is with the distinctive character of the sequence at Tara that this chapter ends.

Tara has not been extensively excavated and what work has been carried out has yet to be fully published. On the other hand, recent years have seen an extensive programme of topographical and geophysical survey which have done much to elucidate the character and chronology of the separate monuments on the site (Newman 1997). That has run in parallel with a systematic study of the documentary evidence concerned with the later importance of the monuments (Bhreathnach 1995). The summary that follows is based on that work but necessarily simplifies some of the detail.

The use of Tara can be divided into three broad developments (Newman 1997). The first traces its history from a Neolithic enclosure to the creation of a barrow cemetery of Bronze Age date. The second concerns developments during the Iron Age when many of the older remains were incorporated in a more complex arrangement of monuments. This was the time when Tara was a royal centre, comparable with others in Ireland, such as Navan Fort. Finally, there is the early medieval period in which the site achieved its lasting fame in Irish literature. We know something of its historical significance and the ways in which it was used, but at present there is little to suggest that new structures were still being built.

The first sequence has much in common with the groups of earlier prehistoric monuments discussed in the previous chapter (Figure 5. 15). Almost every earthwork on the site seems to have been created in response to what was there before, and with each new phase of activity existing structures were reused or rebuilt.

The first activity at Tara is probably represented by a Neolithic palisaded enclosure, not unlike other examples in Ireland. Too little of this survives to permit any detailed discussion, but it may be significant that part of its perimeter was overlain by a passage grave, associated with a large number of cremation burials. There may have been a monolith of white granite in front of the entrance to the tomb. The newly built passage grave seems to have been located just beyond the terminal of a cursus, but this interpretation needs to be tested by excavation. Yet another enclosure has recently been identified by geophysical survey (Newman 1999). This consists of two rows of pits separated by a ditch and seems to be some kind of henge. The chronological relationship between these different features is by no means obvious. The cursus might have been directed towards the first enclosure on the site or, alternatively, it could have been contemporary with the passage grave. What is clear is that the henge monument has a rather elliptical outline, instead of the more standard circular ground plan. This may have happened because it needed to respect the position of the cursus to the north and to incorporate the passage grave to the south. There is a second henge a kilometre away, and these monuments may have formed only part of a larger ceremonial complex. At all events, the Hill of Tara juxtaposes each of the major Neolithic structures found in Ireland: an early enclosure, a megalithic tomb, a cursus and a henge.

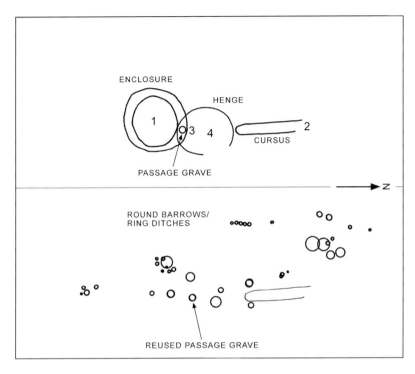

ENCLOSURE

HENGE

1

3 4

CURSUS

2

PASSAGE GRAVE

N

ROUND BARROWS/
RING DITCHES

REUSED PASSAGE GRAVE

Figure 5.15 Diagram summarising the relationships between the earlier prehistoric monuments at the 'royal' site of Tara, Ireland. The upper drawing shows the situation during the Neolithic period and the lower diagram outlines the reorganisation of the site during the Bronze Age. The numbers in the upper drawing indicate one possible sequence of construction.

Source: information from Newman (1997 and 1999).

More monuments were built around this original nucleus. Newman (1997) suggests that two round barrows continued the axis formed by the cursus and the passage grave, and another group of three was built elsewhere on the site during the Bronze Age. It was during this period that the megalithic tomb was reused. Inhumation burials were placed inside the Neolithic structure and a large number of cremations were inserted in its covering mound. Excavation of these burials produced grave goods of exceptional quality. The Middle Bronze Age also saw the deposition of some notable artefacts at Tara, although little is known about their original contexts. They include three gold torcs, two ear rings and a bronze rapier. Newman suggests that many more round barrows were built at about the same time. A cluster of mounds or ring ditches was located towards the end of the cursus, while some of the others extended its alignment.

By this stage Tara was an important barrow cemetery, but, as so often, the positions of those barrows were related to those of monuments surviving from the past. The passage grave was brought back into use to receive an unusually large number of burials, and the axis originally established by the cursus may have retained some of its importance, although the widening distribution of mounds across the hilltop suggests that the orderly pattern established in the Neolithic period was gradually breaking down.

The second stage in the history of Tara was during the Iron Age when it took on all the attributes of a royal centre (Figure 5.16). The main feature to be built was a large enclosure with an external bank and an internal ditch (Ráith na Rig). Although it once seemed possible that this was another henge, recent excavation has shown that its bank overlies the remains of an iron working furnace (Roche 1999). It is better compared with other earthworks of this type which occur at ceremonial sites of the late prehistoric period. The enclosure had been carefully

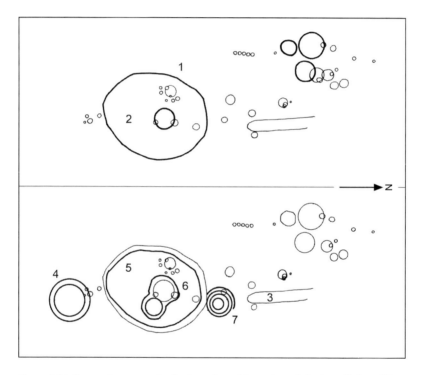

Figure 5.16 Successive stages in the Iron Age elaboration of the 'royal' site of Tara, Ireland. The upper diagram summarises the first group of monuments to be created and the lower drawing shows the complex at its fullest development.

Source: information from Newman (1997).

Key
1: Ráith na Rig; 2: large central mound; 3: reused cursus; 4: Ráith Lógaire; 5: the recreation of the Ráith na Rig as a defended site; 6: the recreation of the central mound as a ringfort (Tech Cormaic); 7: Rath of the Synods.

positioned in relation to the older monuments on the hill. It cut across the edge of the henge identified by geophysics and incorporated the remains of the passage grave within its perimeter. It seems to have included a number of round barrows and was positioned approximately in line with the cursus.

In Newman's interpretation, which is supported by the unpublished excavations of the 1950s, a major circular enclosure (the Rath of the Synods) was one of the next features to be constructed on the site. It was built against the outer bank of the Ráith na Ríg and was located directly opposite the remains of the passage grave that had been included within that monument. It is known that the Rath of the Synods went through a number of periods of use and that at different times its interior was occupied by burials and timber buildings. Newman (1997) argues that a less elaborate circular earthwork (Ráith Lógaire) was constructed on the opposite side of the large enclosure. In between them, in the centre of Ráith na Ríg, a circular mound was formed over the remains of earlier round barrows.

It was inside that great arena that the last earthworks at Tara were built. The existing mound within its circuit was reconstructed on a more elaborate scale, and a ringfort was built beside it. The two earthworks were joined together to form a single design. During the same phase, Newman suggests, the Ráith na Ríg was reconstructed as a defensive monument.

In its Iron Age form Tara has all the attributes of a royal centre, and indeed it is described in that way in the earliest written sources. It includes a prominent mound, suitable for the inauguration of a new ruler, and it also has a large enclosure with an internal ditch. The Rath of the Synods is defined by four concentric earthworks – an unusual feature on any site in Ireland – and the wooden buildings inside it take the same form as those excavated at Navan Fort and other ceremonial enclosures of the Iron Age (Cooney and Grogan 1994: figure 10. 2; Waterman 1997). What is particularly interesting about Tara is the extent to which its importance was rooted in a distant past. The layout of the royal site was determined by the axis of a number of Neolithic and Bronze Age earthworks which were still visible on the hilltop, and these seem to have been treated with respect. The Rath of the Synods was built at the end of the Neolithic cursus, and the principal enclosure known as the Ráith na Ríg was designed to include the passage grave within its area. The circular earthwork described as Ráith Lógaire is on the same alignment as the cursus and the passage grave, while the great mound at the centre of this complex may have incorporated the remains of older Bronze Age barrows. Every effort was made to accommodate what survived from the past. This happened to such an extent that it must have been to that link with the past that the kings of Tara owed some of their power. It was only when that power was threatened, at the very end of the sequence, that the first defences were constructed on the site.

The final phase in the history of Tara introduces some quite new issues. It is clear that the site was used throughout the second half of the first millennium AD, but there is no indication that new monuments were built during this time, nor are there many artefacts dating from the period. Ironically, this is when Tara became famous in early Irish literature.

The written sources identify Tara as a place inhabited by the gods, a sacred location which provided access to another world. It was here that divine kings ensured the fertility of the land and new rulers were inaugurated. The hill provided the setting for great public assemblies, and those rulers enjoyed special status among the kings of early Ireland. In legend it was where Saint Patrick converted King Lóegaire to Christianity. In the early Middle Ages, different groups sought to advance their claims to power by emphasising their ancestral links to Tara. In the end, the hill achieved a special position as the seat of the High Kings of Ireland. It retained its legendary importance even after it lost its pre-eminent position to Dublin in the eleventh century, but the only new structure to be built there was a Christian church, which was in existence by 1212.

It is not clear how far these sources describe what really happened, but it does seem likely that the site was used in these ways for a significant period after the last earthwork monuments had been built. If that is true, then the Hill of Tara enters Irish history some time after its visible archaeology comes to an end. The final stages in its development were apparently played out in a landscape made up entirely of ancient monuments (Table 5.2).

Table 5.2 An interpretation of the archaeological sequence at Tara, emphasising (in italics) those elements that seem to refer back to the past history of the site

---

FIRST CYCLE (Neolithic and Bronze Age)

1 Building of palisaded enclosure, passage grave, cursus and henge.

2 *Reuse of passage grave.* Construction of round barrows and ring ditches, *some of them on the axis of the cursus.*

HIATUS? (Later Bronze Age)

Deposition of metalwork among the existing monuments?

SECOND CYCLE (Iron Age)

1 Building of main enclosure *incorporating the position of the passage grave.* Creation of a large mound in the centre of the enclosure. *Reuse of the cursus as a 'road' leading into the main enclosure. Creation of two smaller circular enclosures on the axis of the cursus.*

2 Elaboration of the central mound and construction of a ring fort within the main enclosure. Addition of defences to the main enclosure.

3 Construction of earthworks ends.

THIRD CYCLE (Early Medieval)

1 *Reinterpretation of earthwork monuments in oral and written traditions.*

2 *Construction of a Christian church.*

A summary

In the first part of this chapter I used the archaeology of the Roman and Medieval periods to investigate some of the motives behind the reuse of ancient monuments. Although there are many unsolved problems, three processes seemed to be especially important: interpretation, confrontation and legitimation.

The second part of the chapter explored the reuse of prehistoric sites, although the histories of some of these places extended into the early Middle Ages. I began with regional studies of monument reuse in North Germany, and then offered more detailed analyses at two different scales. I compared the relationship between La Tène funerary enclosures and older monuments on either side of the English Channel, before ending with a short account of the evolution of the Irish royal site at Tara. What can we conclude from this exercise?

In North Germany, it was possible to compare two rather different accounts of much the same evidence: Holtorf's 'biography' of megaliths and Sopp's less theoretical analysis of a larger sample of mortuary monuments. Both were sufficient to show that people had a keen awareness of the remains of the ancient past and were highly selective in the kinds of structure that they sought to reuse, but the evidence was so varied that it was hard to offer a simple explanation of such extensive patterns.

The second study focused on a more specific relationship: that between La Tène funerary enclosures and the other monuments with which they were associated. In Continental Europe, their appearance may signify the adoption of new religious beliefs, but the monuments themselves were frequently constructed within already existing cemeteries. Only occasionally was this impossible, and in that case there was a preference for linking the new kinds of earthwork to the remains of Bronze Age or Early Iron Age barrows whose original uses could still have been recalled. In England, on the other hand, barrow building had lapsed many centuries earlier and here it seems as if the square enclosures were much more closely linked to the monuments of a remote past. Except in North-East England, there seems to have been the same conceptual link between these earthworks and round barrows, but in this case it could only be established by reference to structures of considerable antiquity whose original significance would have been long forgotten. This may have invested the development of a new form of ritual site with the authority of the past.

Tara is even more informative. Here all the processes defined in the first part of the chapter are in evidence. There is no doubt that the Iron Age royal capital was formed out of the surviving remains of earlier prehistoric monuments and must have gained some of its power from doing so, just as it is no accident that one of the richest cemeteries in Early Bronze Age Ireland should have involved the reuse of a Neolithic passage grave on the site. In the same way, there is historical evidence that during the first millennium AD different groups were seeking to advance their own positions by emphasising, and even fabricating, their links with Tara.

There is also evidence of confrontation, although this is much more limited. It seems unlikely that Saint Patrick ever visited the site, but Newman has suggested that the final stage in the elaboration of the royal complex coincides with the decline of paganism and the arrival of the Christian religion. At this stage, the construction of ceremonial monuments ended, and the last features to be built seem to have been defences of an entirely secular character. This change could be echoed in Irish tradition, which tells that in the sixth century AD Saint Rúadán cursed Duarmait mac Cerball, the king of Tara, for carrying out pagan ceremonies on the hill. Another case of confrontation may be the construction of the early Medieval church beside the Rath of the Synods. This happened after the active life of the site was over but during a period when its past history played an increasing role in Irish literature.

Lastly, there is considerable evidence of interpretation. A group of round barrows was rebuilt as a single mound that may have been used for inaugurations. The cursus seems to have been adopted as a monumental approach to the Ráith na Rig and the Rath of the Synods, and was presumably seen in the same light as the 'royal droveways' found on Iron Age sites of similar status (Wailes 1982). The standing stone that may have stood outside the passage grave came to symbolise the fertility of the kingdom and the union of the ruler and his land.

The same process went on after Tara had been abandoned and is epitomised by the prose text *Dindgnai Temrach* (Tara's remarkable places), composed in the twelfth century AD (Bhreathnach 1995). This draws on the history and legends associated with the site, yet it also provides a surprisingly accurate reconstruction of the nature and location of the different monuments there. Indeed, it is so accurate that it was possible for Petrie to make direct use of it in his survey of the remains published in 1839. His was one of the first pieces of analytical fieldwork carried out in Ireland, but it was by no means the earliest, for the author(s) of the Medieval text must have undertaken a similar exercise. There was no direct evidence to show them how the various monuments had been used, and it was necessary to match the traditional stories to *the physical remains* of the earthworks that survived on the hill. It was an endeavour that takes us back to the very beginnings of field archaeology.

That reference to the early development of archaeology also brings us back to some of the issues considered in the first chapter of this book. I return to them one last time before this study ends.

Chapter 6

Conclusion

Prehistoric times

At Stourhead

If Darwin's travels in the 1830s were one turning point in the recognition of prehistory, so, a generation earlier, were the Napoleonic Wars. This was because of the way in which they restricted access to the Mediterranean.

Like Darwin, Sir Richard Colt Hoare was a great traveller in the first part of his life, but there the similarity ends. They came from very different backgrounds. Darwin's grandfather had been famous as a doctor, as well as a poet, inventor and scientist (King-Hele 1968). Colt Hoare's grandfather, on the other hand, was a successful banker and is remembered today as the creator of the famous landscape garden at Stourhead (Woodbridge 1970: chapter 1). Sir Richard inherited that estate, but some of his early years were spent abroad, visiting the Classical world. Indeed, in 1819 he even published a book entitled *A Classical Tour through Italy and Sicily*, but by then he was also organising a campaign of excavation on the Wessex chalk that laid the foundations for the study of prehistoric Britain (Woodbridge 1970: parts 2–4; Annable and Simpson 1964: 1–6)

That change of direction is worth exploring in more detail. His grandfather, Henry Hoare, had created the gardens at Stourhead in the middle of the eighteenth century and had built a house there. It is impossible to understand either project without appreciating the different ways in which they referred to the past.

The house was built in the English Palladian style. That is to say, it was closely modelled on the buildings in Italy designed by Andrea Palladio nearly 200 years before. In turn, these were influenced by Classical principles, and the very idea of a rural villa owed much to ancient writers. Henry Hoare was living in a Roman country house.

The landscape that he created at Stourhead was indebted to rather similar sources. On one level it was influenced by the seventeenth century paintings of Claude Lorrain and Poussin, both of whom depicted landscapes from antiquity. Stourhead has many of the same elements: groups of trees, a deep valley, a lake and distant views of hills. There are Classical temples and a grotto (Figure 6.1). Indeed, Woodbridge has suggested a specific source for part of the design in

Figure 6.1 View of the landscape at Stourhead, Southern England.

Claude Lorrain's painting, 'Aeneas at Delos' (1970: 33 and plate 2b). The comparison does not end there, for Stourhead also features a number of statues based on ancient models and even includes two inscriptions quoting passages from Virgil. Every part of that landscape was meant to be viewed from a particular direction, and each of these features was to be contemplated in turn, so that they could be taken together to compose a narrative. Woodbridge suggests that the story in question is that of the *Aeneid*, and this seems to be confirmed in a letter written by Hoare himself (ibid.: 33–6).

Why was it important to make that specific connection? There are two possible reasons. It may have a personal reference. To quote Beardsley's account:

> The visual and psychological complexity achieved [by the layout of Stourhead] is underscored by a rich and apparently autobiographical programme. Over the entrance to the grotto is an inscription from Book I of the *Aeneid*; another from Book II is in the Temple of Flora. The circuit walk around the lake may have been intended as an allegory of Aeneas's travels, with particular reference to his descent into the underworld to see his father, which began at Lake Avernus. Hoare's only son had died in 1751, so he may have felt especially inspired to evoke this story of the reunion of father and son.
>
> (1989: 65)

Woodbridge offers a simpler explanation. Perhaps Hoare 'was celebrating the founding of Rome, just as he, like Aeneas, was establishing his family in a place' (1970: 36). That idea recalls the discussion of origin myths in Chapter 2. The same applies to a monument at Stourhead which does not refer to the Roman world. Instead, it is a brick tower dedicated to King Alfred. Although it was built to commemorate a war with Spain, Woodbridge suggests that this might also be connected with the story told by Geoffrey of Monmouth that the Kings of England were descended from the grandson of Aeneas (ibid.: 36). This is by no means certain, as Hoare developed a taste for the Gothic in later life and added other Medieval elements to the original design at Stourhead.

It was the references to the Classical world that caught the imagination of his grandson. Surrounded by so many images of antiquity, it is hardly surprising that Richard Colt Hoare was deeply involved with the culture of ancient Rome. After the death of his wife when he was just 27, he travelled extensively on the Continent, making only one visit to England in 6 years. His journeys took him to Italy, Sicily, Spain, Switzerland, Germany and Malta, and during that time he acquired an appetite for original research and began to investigate the cities of the Etruscans (ibid.: part 2). When he came home, conditions in France had reached a crisis and there was no realistic prospect of returning to parts of Continental Europe for many years.

Forced to confine his activities to the British Isles, Colt Hoare turned to the very different landscape of Wales and took an interest in Medieval history and architecture, but at last more local research attracted his attention. This was due to the work of William Cunnington, who had embarked on a series of excavations at prehistoric burial mounds in Wiltshire. Soon Colt Hoare became involved in this scheme. He funded the investigation of the barrows, commissioned a series of earthwork surveys and organised the publication of the project. The result was the compilation of a record which is still used today (Annable and Simpson 1964: 1–6; Piggott 1989: 153–7).

Thus it came about that one of the earliest and most sustained programmes of prehistoric archaeology was conducted by someone who had been formed in a completely different tradition of scholarship. He lived in what was essentially a Roman villa, on the edge of a landscape whose layout was inspired by the writings of Virgil. His park was designed to look like a seventeenth century painting, and yet he devoted his research to the earthworks and graves of people who had inhabited the same region 4000 years before.

Colt Hoare's excavations at the burial mounds of Wiltshire broke with tradition just as Darwin's work departed from orthodox notions of human antiquity. Both men had important predecessors, and yet within a few decades the key elements of a prehistoric archaeology were in place: Darwin's thinking demanded an extended time scale, reaching back far beyond the period of the first written records, and the research of Colt Hoare and Cunnington posed the problem of forming a history entirely from material remains. Cut off from the sites that he had known on the Continent, Colt Hoare devoted himself to a new kind of archaeology. That interruption in his own career symbolises a wider development in the discipline.

Renewing the past

It is important to understand why these changes were significant. There is the question of time. As long as he remained involved in the study of Mediterranean culture, Colt Hoare had a ready-made chronology to hand. Part of it was based on the writings of historians and on the sequence of Roman emperors. It was also calibrated by a series of well documented events. He would not have found this difficult to understand, for it could be translated into the terms with which he was familiar: the continuous unfolding of time in a single sequence leading from the past to the present. In Chapter 1 I emphasised that this is the conception of time that dominates in a mercantile economy. What could be more appropriate for an archaeologist whose family owned a bank?

There would have been other time scales with which Colt Hoare was acquainted. One was the timeless history of the gods, celebrated in the myths and legends that formed a mainstay of Roman literature. Almost by definition, this reached back to the beginning of creation. Even more important was the origin myth of Rome itself. This was codified in an epic poem, the *Aeneid*, and formed a link between the founding of the city and the story of the Trojan War. His grandfather had made use of the same narrative in structuring his park at Stourhead. This theme seems to have been selected for its autobiographical resonance, although it is worth remembering that in the Middle Ages the same origin myth was elaborated to explain the descent of the English royal house.

The prehistoric remains investigated by Colt Hoare made other demands on his imagination. It was possible to show that individual monuments in Wessex were of pre-Roman origin simply because they were cut by Roman roads, but thereafter his research could only be guided by the physical remains surviving from the past: the monuments he surveyed, the barrows he excavated, and the groups of artefacts he found there. Eventually, archaeologists working in the late nineteenth and early twentieth centuries would be able to reduce this information to order and to provide a more rounded account than Colt Hoare could possibly have done. Their work focused on the sequence of distinctive earthworks in Wessex and on the relationship between the burial mounds and their contents (Piggott 1938). It was especially important to establish a sequence for these grave assemblages in relation to similar material on the Continent. But for Colt Hoare himself this would not have been conceivable. Many years had to pass before it would be possible to work out the chronological intervals between the different finds from his excavations. He was faced with a sequence of uncertain length, in which human activities had changed at a pace that he was unable to calculate. Prehistory was not just about an absence of written sources: its study demanded a new approach to time.

In exactly the same way, Colt Hoare was committed to the recording of material things, even though they lacked any literary associations. That was no mean task, for he was brought up in a tradition, epitomised by the design of Stourhead, in which specific artefacts and monuments made immediately identifiable references to Classical culture. In publishing Bronze Age grave goods he had no such sources to guide him. He recognised this from the outset, and that explains the motto of his life's work: 'We speak from facts not theory'.

That motto sums up the character of Colt Hoare's research. He was primarily concerned with collecting and organising data. He illustrated many of the artefacts from his excavations and he made arrangements for their curation, so that they remain available for study even now. In another sense, the motto is unfortunate. Not only does it suggest that excavators recover facts, unaffected by their preconceptions and expectations, it also implies that theorising on the basis of that material is to be discouraged. His project was originally conceived as a contribution to a 'History' of Wiltshire, but the publication actually provides a *description* of prehistoric artefacts and their contexts. It would be 100 years before Piggott (1938) could use that same information to establish their antiquity.

The reason for that delay was the necessity of devising methods which allowed material culture to play a central part in the narrative, and this is the other key to the development of prehistory. Not only does this subject operate on different time scales from most historical studies, it employs quite different sources of information. Many historians do take account of material culture, but prehistorians are necessarily cut off from any access to documents. It was the work of Childe, a century after Colt Hoare, that provided an explicit methodology for writing about the human past on the basis of physical remains. Only then were Colt Hoare's 'facts' readily translatable into theories.

The past in field archaeology: the vertical and the horizontal

This book began with the career of Darwin and concludes with the work of Colt Hoare. The fact they were near-contemporaries, living in the same country, is incidental. I have chosen these two figures because their work epitomises quite different strands in the development of prehistory.

Darwin's writings have had a profound influence over the ways in which archaeologists conduct their work. This is partly because he demonstrated the antiquity of the human species, but it is also because of the methods by which he and his contemporaries were able to measure time. Darwin was influenced by geology, and it was the fossil record that provided the most convincing evidence for his account of evolution. From his observations of living creatures, Darwin could postulate some of the mechanisms behind the origin of species, but only the fossil record could trace their course over long periods of time.

That same emphasis on measuring sequence has been influential in the development of prehistoric archaeology and, in particular, in the establishment of field techniques. Here a key figure is General Pitt Rivers (Thompson 1977; Bowden 1991). He employed a geological model in his excavations, so that he could measure the evolution of ancient material culture in relation to the stratigraphies he encountered in the field. His famous Relic Tables purport to be an objective record of what was found (Pitt Rivers 1887–98), just as Colt Hoare recorded the artefacts from different barrows in Wiltshire; but Pitt Rivers' real agenda was to treat portable objects as if they were biological organisms which had evolved over long periods of time. He argued that ancient artefacts developed according to similar principles to living creatures and underwent the same process of natural selection, although in this case the survival of the fittest was governed by utility: those inventions that performed better than their counterparts contributed more to the evolution of material culture. In his writings he related the character of ancient objects to the layers in which they were found. In that way he could complement the conjectural histories of these forms based on ethnographic sources (Lucas 2001: 19–26).

Pitt Rivers employed a geological framework for his excavations, but behind it lay a more theoretical programme. If he could show that ancient material culture followed the same principles as Darwinian evolution, he might be able to demonstrate that changes in human society happened extremely slowly. Pitt Rivers was influenced by the 'social Darwinism' of Spencer and concluded that sudden change was incompatible with the natural order (Bradley 1984). He tried to enter politics, but without success, and created his own museums in order to teach this message. Thus Darwin's work influenced the ways in which the archaeological record was perceived and also contributed to the interpretation of society as a whole.

These influences extended into the twentieth century. The study of social organisation became one of the key elements in the growth of processual archaeology, and the conjectural histories proposed by anthropologists like Service and Fried have had an enormous influence. But it is in field archaeology that Darwin's legacy is paramount. In the first half of the twentieth century a number of excavators, notably Wheeler, reinforced the General's emphasis on the stratigraphic sequence as the key to any field investigation. In his account of field archaeology Wheeler (1954) overlooked the theoretical agenda behind Pitt Rivers' work and, like many of his contemporaries, treated him simply as a brilliant technician. Indeed, such was the emphasis on establishing a stratigraphic succession – from Palaeolithic cave sediments to the defences of Iron Age hill forts – that it was often very difficult to appreciate the range of variation in past activity. What is curious is that even with the adoption of more extensive excavations this obsession with the vertical sequence still has so much influence.

This can be seen both in field reports and in the recording of excavations (Lucas 2001: chapter 5). One of the key tools is the stratigraphic matrix, which expresses in diagrammatic form the chronological relationship between all the deposits encountered during that work. Indeed, this technique has provided the subject for an entire book (Harris 1989) and threatens to overwhelm any account of field techniques. This is not to deny the importance of stratigraphy, but to emphasise that it necessarily implies a conception of time akin to Darwinian evolution. It provides a single scale that proceeds inexorably from the past to the present, and in that sense excavation records reproduce modern Western ideas of time and how it is measured. That is especially clear from the publication of major field projects in which the stratigraphic matrix and the sequence of arte-facts still seem to dominate other aspects of the work.

This sits uneasily with two features of stratigraphic excavation. It does not do enough justice to 'cut' or 'negative' features, and it places too little weight on residuality among the artefacts that come from these projects. Cut features such as ditches or pits interrupt the progressive accumulation of layers, and these must be recognised if the sequence is to be read correctly. Such elements may play a significant part in the history of the site, but one reason for defining them so precisely is that they intrude into earlier levels and may contain older material recycled from those deposits. That material is useless as dating evidence and for that reason it is described as 'residual'. It has to be eliminated from any attempt to establish the age of the excavated structures.

But there is another way of considering this relationship. Very few prehistoric sites conform to the geological model that has been inherited from the nineteenth century. The successive surfaces are cut by features that reach down into earlier deposits and bring older material to the surface in the same manner as a modern excavation. The comparison goes even further, for these same features provide one way in which ancient artefacts are revealed to later generations. Even in prehistory, people must have been aware of this phenomenon. The stratigraphic sequence recorded on so many excavations is interrupted by 'fissures' that extend into older deposits; and these can be considered as *channels* that open between the present and the past. Such observations have always posed a problem for interpretation, and yet contemporary archaeologists have devised working pro-cedures which allow this question to be ignored.

If Darwin's work influenced the way in which archaeology would develop, this is also true of Colt Hoare, whose career straddled three different worlds. So far I have discussed the way in which his research changed from the visual and literary culture of the Roman period to the portable artefacts of prehistory. It is important to remember that he was also a pioneer of field survey. Again he had a talented collaborator, in this case Philip Crocker (Woodbridge 1970: 210–17). Together they recorded many of the surviving earthworks on the Wessex downland. It is due to their efforts that so many features were identified before their destruction by modern farming. Although they were not the first people to undertake this kind of research, it was many years before their initiative would be matched by a new generation of fieldwork.

The barrows excavated by Colt Hoare and Cunnington feature in some of these surveys, but there were many other sites as well, including field systems, land boundaries, hill forts, settlements and enclosures. The fact that they could still be recognised as earthworks in the early nineteenth century makes another important point about the archaeologist's notion of time.

In contrast to the 'vertical' model that derives from geology, field survey emphasises the 'horizontal' axis. It is concerned with mapping the remains of past activity over an extensive area. That is not to deny the value of establishing chronological relationships. It is of vital importance to determine the order in which particular features of the landscape developed, and this is often achieved by working out a structural sequence based on intersecting earthworks. The process is not unlike excavation, but with the 'vertical' element removed.

Field survey depends entirely on the continued visibility of the remains of the past. Far from being buried, they are apparent on the surface. The passage of time has not concealed these elements: rather, it has led to their proliferation, and the task of the archaeologist is to reduce such complex evidence to its basic outlines (Bowden 1999). The results of ancient activity would have been visible to people in prehistory just as they can still be identified today. That applies just as much to ancient buildings, like those Colt Hoare encountered in the Mediterranean, as it does to the earthwork monuments that he recorded on the English downland; and because such evidence was always exposed to scrutiny, it draws together the traces of very different times. The image of archaeological excavation is that it brings something hidden to view. Field survey compares phenomena of different ages that have fused together between the moment of their creation and their appearance in the present.

The same contrast would have been important in antiquity. Portable material culture may have circulated long after its production because some items had been regarded as heirlooms and others had been rediscovered after they were first deposited. That would not have been true of the ways in which people in the past modified the appearance of the land, by building earthworks or by other projects. These were always present and would have posed a problem to later generations. In fact their very survival presented several choices: they could be ignored or even destroyed, or their significance would need to be interpreted. Their physical fabric might even be renewed. This is not a simple matter of 'continuity', but results from strategic decisions that may have been made long after the original roles of these features had been forgotten. In principle, each excavated context provides a snapshot of one particular moment. Where surface remains survived in the wider landscape, the products of many different ages would have presented themselves simultaneously, and it would have been quite impossible to adhere to a strictly linear notion of time. The landscape is where different time scales intersect, and archaeologists have always accepted that. What they tend to forget is that this was equally true for people in prehistory who would also have come to terms with these traces of the past.

I have contrasted two of the ways in which archaeologists can think about the past by comparing different kinds of fieldwork. I have associated each of them with a tradition that was practised in the nineteenth century; indeed, the history of topographical survey goes back even further. Each of these methods implies a particular idea of time. Excavation is based on the succession of deposits, and field survey on a gradual accumulation of features on the surface. Thus in the first case time is singular and one deposit follows another. In the second example, times are multiple and overlapping, so that the groups of earthworks surveyed by Colt Hoare in Wiltshire may have accumulated over hundreds of years. It is this conception of the past that is better suited to archaeological analysis. Earlier chapters have illustrated some of the ways in which people in prehistory made use of such an inheritance.

Coda: the garden of time

I have borrowed the title of this section from a story by J. G. Ballard (1984). This is not about prehistory, but such an evocative description could well be applied to Colt Hoare's park at Stourhead.

Earlier I described the ideas behind the creation of Stourhead and the ways in which they were indebted to Classical and Medieval sources. It was in this form that they passed from Henry Hoare to his grandson and did so much to colour his attitudes to the past.

There is a quite different sense in which the layout of the gardens provides an image of archaeology itself: an image that emphasises that discipline's distinctive approach to time. At Stourhead, the visual culture of different periods comes together in a single design. There are Classical statues, but there is also a Medieval cross. There are pagan temples in the park, but at the head of the lake is a modern village. At one time the Classical structures were complemented by a ruined nunnery built in the Gothic manner, and the house in which Colt Hoare came to live combined sixteenth century architecture with a much more ancient prototype. The house was a reinterpretation of the rural villas described by Roman writers, just as the layout of the park was influenced by paintings of antiquity. On one level, this demonstrates how that past could be recreated and reused. On another, the landscape at Stourhead stands for a different characteristic of the archaeological record.

Although Colt Hoare's collection of antiquities from Wiltshire barrows was once displayed in his house, the surrounding landscape refers mainly to the Roman past. It can also serve as an image of the prehistoric period, for around the margins of the lake monuments of quite different ages are artfully juxtaposed. In order to understand them, we do not trace each structure back to its original source of inspiration, for the links between these buildings amount to more than the sum of the separate parts. At Stourhead, the emblems of different ages are brought together, so that this was truly a garden of time. It was a place where life was lived with an awareness of many different pasts and where those pasts reached out to meet the present. The same was often true in prehistoric times, and this book has attempted to say something about how that happened.

Bibliography

Adam, B. 1990 *Time and Social Theory*, Cambridge: Polity Press.

Anati, E. 1968 *Arte rupestre nella regione occidental della Peninsula Iberica*, Brescia: Archivi di Arti Preistorica.

André, J. 1961 'Les dolmens morbihanais remployés à l'époque romaine', *Ogam* 75: 248–54.

Annable, K. and Simpson, D. 1964 *Guide Catalogue to the Neolithic and Bronze Age Collections in Devizes Museum*, Devizes: Wiltshire Archaeological Society.

Appadurai, A. (ed.) 1986 *The Social Life of Things*, Cambridge: Cambridge University Press.

Ars, E. 1997 'Les figurines gallo-romaines en terre cuite en Morbihan', *Bulletin et Memories de la Société Polymathique du Morbihan* 123: 41–54.

Ashwin, T. and Bates, S. 2000 'Excavations on the Norwich Southern Bypass: Part 1', *East Anglian Archaeology* 91.

Bailey, D. 2000 *Balkan Prehistory*, London: Routledge.

Bailloud, G., Boujot, C., Cassen, S. and Le Roux, C.-T. 1995 *Carnac. Les premières architectures de pierre*, Paris: CNRS.

Bakels, C. 1978 'Four Linearbandkeramik settlements and their environment', *Analecta Praehistorica Leidensia* 11.

Ballard, J. G. 1984 'The garden of time', in J. G. Ballard, *The Voices of Time*, pp. 115–23, London: Jonathan Cape.

Baray, L., Le Goff, I., Thébault, D. and Villeneur, I. 1994 'La nécropole de Soucy/Mocques Bouteilles', in L. Baray, S. Deffresigne, C. Leroyer and I. Villeneur (eds), *Nécropoles protohistoriques du Séonais*, pp. 84–171, Paris: Editions des Sciences de l'Homme.

Barber, L. 1980 *The Heyday of Natural History 1820–1870*, London: Jonathan Cape.

Barclay, A. and Harding, J. (eds) 1999 *Pathways and Ceremonies: the Cursus Monuments of Britain and Ireland*, Oxford: Oxbow.

Barfield, L. 1995 'The context of statue-menhirs', *Notizie Archeologische Bergomensi* 3: 11–20.

Barnatt, J. 1998 'Monuments in the landscape: thoughts from the Peak', in A. Gibson and D. Simpson (eds), *Prehistoric Ritual and Religion*, pp. 92–105, Stroud: Sutton.

Barrett, J. 1999 The mythical landscape of the British Iron Age, in W. Ashmore and A. B. Knapp (eds), *Archaeologies of Landscape*, pp. 253–65, Oxford: Blackwell.

Bauch, W., Clausen, I., Kramer, W. and Kuhn, H.-J. 1989 'Sechster Arbeitsbericht des Landesantes für Vor- und Frügeschichte von Schleswig-Holstein. Grabungs-berichteder Jahre 1978–1979', *Offa* 46: 333–98.

Beardsley, J. 1989 *Earthworks and Beyond. Contemporary Art in the Landscape*, New York: Abbeville Press.

Bhreathnach, E. 1995 'The topography of Tara: the documentary evidence', *Discovery Programme Reports* 2: 68–77.

Billard, C., Carré, F., Guillon, M. and Treffort 1998 'L'occupation funéraire des monuments mégalithiques pendant la haut moyen age. Modalités et essai d'interpretation', *Bulletin de la Société préhistorique Française* 93: 279–86.

Binford, L. 1965 'Archaeological systematics and the study of culture process', *American Antiquity* 31: 203–10.

Birdwell-Pheasant, D. and Lawrence-Zuñiga, D. (eds) 1999 *House Life. Space and Family in Europe*, Oxford: Berg.

Bittel, K. 1998 *Die keltischen Viereckschanzen*, Stuttgart: Theiss.

Blair, J. 1995 'Anglo-Saxon pagan shrines and their prototypes', *Anglo-Saxon Studies in Archaeology and History* 8: 1–28.

Boston, R. 1975 *The Admirable Urquart*, London: Fraser.

Boujot, C. and Cassen, S. 1993 'A pattern of evolution for the Neolithic funerary structures in the west of France', *Antiquity* 67: 477–91.

Boujot, C. and Cassen, S. 1998 'Tertres armoricains et tertres carnacéens dans le cadre de la néolithisation de la France occidentale', in J. Guilaine (ed.), *Sépultures d'Occident et genèses des mégalithismes*, pp. 107–26, Paris: Errance.

Bourdieu, P. 1977 *Outline of a Theory of Practice*, Cambridge: Cambridge University Press.

Bourgeois, J. 1998 'La nécropole laténienne et Gallo-Romain d'Ursel-Rozenstraat (Flandre orientale, Belgique)', *Revue Archéologique de Picardie* 1: 111–25.

Bowden, M. 1991 *Pitt Rivers*, Cambridge: Cambridge University Press.

Bowden, M. 1999 *Unravelling the Landscape: an Inquisitive Approach to Archaeology*, Stroud: Tempus.

Bradley, R. 1984 'Archaeology, evolution and the public good: the intellectual development of General Pitt Rivers', *Archaeological Journal* 140: 1–9.

Bradley, R. 1988 'Status, wealth and the chronological ordering of cemeteries', *Proceedings of the Prehistoric Society* 54: 327–8.

Bradley, R. 1998 *The Significance of Monuments*, London: Routledge.

Bradley, R. 2000 *The Good Stones. A New Investigation of the Clava Cairns*, Edinburgh: Society of Antiquaries of Scotland.

Bradley, R. 2001 'Orientations and origins: a symbolic dimension to the long house in Neolithic Europe', *Antiquity* 75: 50–8.

Bradley, R., Ball, C., Croft, S., Campbell, M., Phillips, T. and Trevarthen, D. 2000 'Tomnaverie stone circle, Aberdeenshire', *Antiquity* 74: 65–6.

Bradley, R. and Ellison, A. 1975 *Rams Hill: a Bronze Age Defended Enclosure and its Landscape*, Oxford: British Archaeological Reports.

Bradley, R., Entwistle, R. and Raymond, F. 1994 *Prehistoric Land Divisions on Salisbury Plain*, London: English Heritage.

Brainerd, G. 1951 'The place of chronological ordering in archaeological analysis', *American Antiquity* 16: 301–13.

Braudel, F. 1969 *Écrits sur l'histoire*, Paris: Flammarion.

Büchsenschütz, O., Olivier, L. and Aillières, A.-M. (eds) 1989 *Les Viereckschanzen et les enceintes quadrilaterales en Europe celtique*, Paris: Errance.

Bueno Ramirez, P. and de Balbín Behrmann, R. 1997 'Ambiente funerario en la sociedad megalitica ibérica: arte megalítico peninsular', in A. Rodríguez Casal (ed.),

O Neolíttico Atlántico e as origines do megalitismo, pp. 693–718, Santiago de Compostela: Universidade de Santiago de Compostela.

Bueno Ramirez, P. and de Balbín Behrmann, R. 2000 'Art mégalithique et art en plein air. Approches de la définition du territoire pour les groups producteurs de la péninsule ibérique', *L'Anthropologie* 104: 427–58.

Burl, A. 1993 *From Carnac to Callanish. The Prehistoric Stone Rows and Avenues of Britain, Ireland and Brittany*, New Haven, CT: Yale University Press.

Burl, A. 2000 *The Stone Circles of Britain, Ireland and Brittany*, New Haven, CT: Yale University Press.

Butler, J. 1991a *Dartmoor Atlas of Antiquities, Volume 1*, Exeter: Devon Books.

Butler, J. 1991b *Dartmoor Atlas of Antiquities, Volume 2*, Exeter: Devon Books.

Butler, J. 1993 *Dartmoor Atlas of Antiquities, Volume 4*, Exeter: Devon Books.

Butler, J. 1994 *Dartmoor Atlas of Antiquities Exeter, Volume 3*, Exeter: Devon Books.

Butler, J. 1997 *Dartmoor Atlas of Antiquities, Volume 5*, Exeter: Devon Books.

Calado, M. 1997 'Cromlechs alentejanos e arte megalítica', *Brigantium* 10: 289–97.

Calvino, I. 1992 *Six Memos for the New Millennium*, London: Jonathan Cape.

Carré, F. 1993 'Deux habitats et une nécropole à Tournedos-sur-Seine', in D. Cliquet, R. Remy-Watte, V. Guichard and M. Vaginay (eds), *Les Celtes en Normandie*, pp. 55–76, Rennes: Révue Archéologique de l'Ouest Supplément 6.

Carsten, J. and Hugh-Jones, S. (eds) 1995 *About the House: Lévi-Strauss and Beyond*, Cambridge: Cambridge University Press.

Cassen, S. 2000 'Stelae reused in the passage graves of western France: history of research and sexualisation of the carvings', in A. Ritchie (ed.), *Neolithic Orkney in its European Context*, pp. 233–46, Cambridge: McDonald Institute for Archaeological Research.

Champion, T. 1982 'The myth of Iron Age invasions in Ireland', in B. Scott (ed.), *Studies on Early Ireland*, pp. 39–44, Belfast: Association of Young Irish Archaeologists.

Chapman, J. 2000 *Fragmentation in Archaeology. People, Places and Broken Objects in the Prehistory of South-eastern Europe*, London: Routledge.

Chapman, M. 1992 *The Celts: the Construction of a Myth*, Basingstoke: Macmillan.

Childe, V. G. 1956 *Piecing Together the Past*, London: Routledge.

Chippindale, C. 1988 'The invention of words for the idea of "prehistory"', *Proceedings of the Prehistoric Society* 54: 303–14.

Cleal, R. 1988 'The occurrence of drilled holes in Later Neolithic pottery', *Oxford Journal of Archaeology* 7: 139–45.

Collum, V. 1935 *The Tressé Iron Age Megalithic Monument*, Oxford: Oxford University Press.

Connerton, P. 1989 *How Societies Remember*, Cambridge: Cambridge University Press.

Cooney, G. and Grogan, E. 1994 *Irish Prehistory. A Social Perspective*, Dublin: Wordwell.

Corchón, M. S. 1997 *La cueva de La Griega de Pedraza (Segovia)*, Zamora: Junta de Castilla y León.

Coudart, A. 1998 *Architecture et société. L'unité et la variation de la maison danubienne*, Paris: Editions de la Maison des Sciences de l'Homme.

Creighton, J. 2000 *Coins and Power in Late Iron Age Britain*, Cambridge: Cambridge University Press.

Cunliffe, B. 2001 *Facing the Ocean: the Atlantic and its Peoples 8000 BC–AD 1500*, Oxford: Oxford University Press.

Daniel, G. 1972 *Megaliths in History*, London: Thames and Hudson.

Dawson, M. 1996 'Plantation Quarry, Willington: excavations 1988–1991', *Bedfordshire Archaeology* 22: 2–49.

De Marinis, R. 1995 'Le stele antropomorfe di Aosta', *Notizie Archeologische Bergomensi* 3: 213–20.

Demoule, J. P. 1999 *Chronologie et société dans les nécropoles celtiques de la culture Aisne-Marne du VI au IIIe siècle avant notre ère*, Amiens: Revue Archéologique de Picardie numéro special.

Desfossées, Y. 1998 'L'apport des fouilles de sauvetages sur l'autoroute A 16: l'example de la vallée de la Cande', *Histoire et Archéologie du Pas-de-Calais* 15: 10–28.

Desmond, A. and Moore, J. 1991 *Darwin*, Harmondsworth: Penguin.

Fabian, J. 1983 *Time and the Other. How Anthropology Makes its Object*, New York: Columbia University Press.

Fitzpatrick, A. 1997 *Archaeological Excavation on the Route of the A27 Westhampnett Bypass 1989–91, Volume 2*, Salisbury: Wessex Archaeology.

Fleming, A. 1988 *The Dartmoor Reaves*, London: Batsford.

Fokkens, H. 1998 'The Ossen Project. The first decade of excavations at Oss', *Analecta Praehistorica Leidensia* 30.

Fokkens, H. and Roymans, N. (eds) 1991 *Nedezzetingen uit de bronstijd en de ijzertid in de lage landen*, Amersfoort: Rijksdienst voor het Oudheidkundig Bodermonderzoek.

Foster, J. 1986 *The Lexden Tumulus*, Oxford: British Archaeological Reports.

Gallay, A. 1995 'Les stèles anthropomorphes du site mégalithique du Petit-Chasseur à Sion (Valais, Suisse)', *Notizie Archeologische Bergomensi* 3: 167–94.

Galliou, P. 1987 *Les tombes romaines d'Armorique*, Paris: Editions de la Maison des Sciences de l'Homme.

Gamble, C. 1999 *The Palaeolithic Societies of Europe*, Cambridge: Cambridge University Press.

Gell, A. 1992 *The Anthropology of Time*, Oxford: Berg.

Gell, A. 1998 *Art and Agency*, Oxford: Clarendon Press.

Gerritsen, F. 1999 'To build or to abandon. The cultural biography of late prehistoric houses and farmsteads in the southern Netherlands', *Archaeological Dialogues* 6(2): 78–114.

Gibson, A. and Kinnes, I. 1997 'On the urns of a dilemma: radiocarbon and the Peterborough problem', *Oxford Journal of Archaeology* 16: 65–72.

Giot, P. R. 1980 'Souterrains et habitats à l'Age du Fer en Armorique', in *Les Gaules d'Armorique*, pp. 56–61, Rennes: Archéologie de l'Ouest Supplément 3.

Giot, P. R. 1987 *Barnenez, Carn, Guenoc*, Rennes: Université de Rennes.

Giot, P. R., Marguerie, D. and Morzadec, H. 1994 'About the age of the oldest passage graves in Brittany', *Antiquity* 68: 624–8.

Goody, J. 1977 *The Domestication of the Savage Mind*, Cambridge: Cambridge University Press.

Gosden, C. 1994 *Social Being and Time*, Oxford: Blackwell.

Gosden, C. and Lock, G. 1998 'Prehistoric histories', *World Archaeology* 30: 2–12.

Gregg, S. A. 1988 *Foragers and Farmers. Population, Interaction and Agricultural Expansion in Prehistoric Europe*, Chicago, IL: Chicago University Press.

Grinsell, L. 1978 'Dartmoor barrows', *Proceedings of the Devon Archaeological Society* 36: 85–180.

Haggarty, A. 1991 'Machrie Moor, Arran: recent excavations of two stone circles', *Proceedings of the Society of Antiquaries of Scotland* 58: 51–94.

Haldane, J. B. S. 1985 'God-makers', in J. B. S. Haldane, *On Being the Right Size and Other Essays*, pp. 85–100, Oxford: Oxford University Press.

Harris, E. 1989 *Principles of Archaeological Stratigraphy*, Second edition, New York: Academic Press.

Harsema, O. 1992 'Bronze Age habitations and other archaeological remains near Hijken, province of Drenthe, Netherlands', in C. Mordant and A. Richards (eds), *L'habitat et l'occupation du sol à l'age du bronze en Europe*, pp. 77–87, Paris: Editions du Comité des Travaux Historiques et Scientifiques.

Hawkes, C. 1950 'British prehistory halfway though the century', *Proceedings of the Prehistoric Society* 17: 1–15.

Henige, D. 1974 *The Chronology of Oral Tradition: Quest for a Chimera*, Oxford: Clarendon Press.

Herne, A. 1986 'A time and place for the Grimston bowl', in J. Barrett and I. Kinnes (eds), *The Archaeology of Context in the Neolithic and Bronze Age: Recent Trends*, pp. 9–21, Sheffield: Sheffield University Department of Prehistory and Archaeology.

Hodder, I. 1982 *Symbols in Action: Ethnoarchaeological Studies of Material Culture*, Cambridge: Cambridge University Press.

Hodder, I. 1990 *The Domestication of Europe*, Oxford: Blackwell.

Hodder, I. 1993 'The narrative and rhetoric of material culture sequences', *World Archaeology* 25: 268–82.

Holtorf, C. 1998 'The life-histories of megaliths in Mecklenburg-Vorpommern (Germany)', *World Archaeology* 30: 23–38.

Hoskins, J. 1998 *Biographical Objects*, London: Routledge.

Howell, R. 2000 'The demolition of the tetrapylon in Caerleon: an erasure of memory?', *Oxford Journal of Archaeology* 19: 387–95.

Hughes, D. and Trautman, T. (eds) 1995 *Time: Histories and Ethnologies*, Ann Arbor, MI: University of Michigan Press.

Hugh-Jones, C. 1979 *From the Milk River*, Cambridge: Cambridge University Press.

Hunt, A., Shotliff, A. and Woodhouse, J. 1986 'A Bronze Age barrow cemetery and Iron Age enclosure at Holt', *Transactions of the Worcestershire Archaeological Society* 10: 7–46.

Hunter-Anderson, R. 1977 'A theoretical approach to the study of house form', in L. Binford (ed.), *For Theory Building in Archaeology*, pp. 287–315, New York: Academic Press.

Hutton, P. 1993 *History as an Art of Memory*, Hanover, NE: University Press of New England.

Jackson, D. 1995 'Archaeology at Grendon Quarry Northamptonshire, Part 2', *Northamptonshire Archaeology* 26: 3–32.

Jones, S. 1997 *The Archaeology of Ethnicity*, London: Routledge.

Kafka, F. 1963a [1931] 'The Great Wall of China', in F. Kafka, *The Complete Short Stories of Franz Kafka*, pp. 235–48, Harmondsworth: Penguin.

Kafka, F. 1963b [1934] 'The news of the building of the Wall: a fragment', in F. Kafka, *The Complete Short Stories of Franz Kafka*, pp. 148–9, Harmondsworth: Penguin.

Keates, S. 2000 'The ancestralisation of the landscape: monumentality, memory and the rock art of the Copper Age Valcamonica', in G. Nash (ed.), *Signifying Place and Space*, pp. 85–102, Oxford: British Archaeological Reports.

Keeley, L. and Cahen, D. 1987 'Early Neolithic forts and villages in north-east Belgium', *Journal of Field Archaeology* 16: 157–66.

Kind, C.-J. 1989 *Ulm-Eggingen. Die Ausgrabungen 1982 bis 1985 in der bankeramischen Siedlung und de mittelaltlichen Wüstung*, Stuttgart: Theiss.

King-Hele, D. 1968 *The Essential Writings of Erasmus Darwin*, London: McGibbon and Kee.

Kinnes, I., Gibson, A., Ambers, J., Bowman, S., Lees, M. and Boast, R. 1991 'Radiocarbon dating and British Beakers: the British Museum programme', *Scottish Archaeological Review* 8: 35–78.

Kristiansen, K. 1984 'Krieger und Häuptlinge in der Bronzezeit Dänemarks. Ein Beitrag zur Geschichte des bronzezeitlichen Schwertes', *Jahrbuch des Römisch-Germanischen Zentralmuseum Mainz* 31: 187–208.

Küchler, S. 1987 'Malangan: art and memory in a Melanesian society', *Man* 22: 238–55.

Küchler, S. 1999 'The place of memory', in A. Forty and S. Küchler (eds), *The Art of Forgetting*, pp. 53–73, Oxford: Berg.

Laser, R. 1959 'Neolithisch-frühbronzezeitliche Gräber und Slawischer Reihengräber-friedhof bei Cörmigk, Kr. Bernburg', *Ausgrabungen und Funde* 4: 36–42.

Lecerf, T. 1999 *Monte neuf: les pierres droites. Reflections autour les menhirs*, Rennes: Association pour la Diffusion des Recherches Archéologiques dans l'Ouest de la France.

Lecornec, J. 1994 *Le Petit Mont, Arzon*, Rennes: Documents Archéologiques de l'Ouest.

Le Men, R. 1868 'Subterranean chambers at La Tourelle near Quimper, Brittany', *Archaeologia Cambrensis* 14: 293–311.

Le Roux C.-T. 1984 'A propos des fouilles de Gavrinis (Morbihan): nouvelles données sur l'art mégalithique Armoricain', *Bulletin de la Société Préhistorique Française* 81: 240–5.

Le Rouzic, Z. 1930 *Les cromlechs d'Er Lannic, commune d'Arzon*, Vannes: Lafoyle et Lamarzelle.

Le Rouzic, Z. 1932 *Tumulus de Mont St-Michel*, Vannes: Lafoyle et Lamarzelle.

L'Helgouac'h, J. 1965 *Les sepultures mégalithiques en Armorique*, Rennes: Université de Rennes.

L'Helgouac'h, J. 1999 'The megalithic culture of western France – continuity and change in extraordinary architecture', in K. Beinhauser, C. Guksch and S. Kus (eds), *Studien zur Megalithik. Forschunungsstand und ethnoarchäologische Perpspektiven*, pp. 133–45, Weissbach: Beier und Beran.

Longworth, I. 1984 *Collared Urns of the Bronze Age in Great Britain and Ireland*, Cambridge: Cambridge University Press.

Lubbock, J. 1865 *Pre-historic Times*, London: Norgate.

Lubbock, J. 1870 *The Origin of Civilization and the Primitive Condition of Man*, London: Longman, Green and Co.

Lucas, G. 2001 *Critical Approaches to Fieldwork*, London: Routledge.

Lüning, J., Kloos, U. and Albert, S. 1989 'Westliche Nachbarn des bandkeramischen kultur: La Hoguette und Limburg', *Germania* 67: 355–420.

Lüning, J. and Stehli, P. 1994 *Die Bandkeramik in Merzbachtal auf der Aldenhoven Platt*, Bonn: Rheinische Ausgrabungen 36.

Mallory, J. 1995 'Statue-menhirs and Indo-Europeans', *Notizie Archeologische Bergomensi* 3: 67–73.

Marshall, A. 1981 'Environmental adaptation and structural design in axially-pitched long houses from prehistoric Europe', *World Archaeology* 13: 10–23.

Martín Valls, R. 1983 'Las insculturas del castro salmantino de Yecla da Yeltes y sus relaciones con los petroglifos gallegos', *Zephyrus* 36: 217–31.

Martínez García, J. 1995 'Grabados prehistoricos, grabados historicos. Reflexiones sobre un debate a superar', *Revista de Arqueologia* 172: 14–23.

Mattheuser, E. 1991 'Die geographische Austrichtung bandkeramischer Häuser', *Studien zur Siedlungsärchäologie* 1: 1–49.

Menez, Y. 1994 'Les enclose de type "ferme indigène" en Bretagne: quelques réflections issues de treize ans de fouilles', in O. Büchsenschütz and P. Méniel (eds), *Les installations agricoles de l'age du Fer en Ile de France*, pp. 255–76, Paris: Presses de l'Ecole Normal Superieure.

Mezzena, F. 1998a 'Le stele antropomorfe in Europa', in F. Mezzena (ed.), *Dei di pietra: la grande statuaria del III milenio a C*, pp. 14–88, Skira: Regione autonoma Valle d'Aosta.

Mezzena, F. 1998b 'Le stele antropomorfe nell'area megalitica di Aosta', in F. Mezzena (ed.), *Dei di pietra: la grande statuaria del III milenio a C*, pp. 91–121, Skira: Regione autonoma Valle d'Aosta.

Midgley, M. 1992 *TRB Culture*, Edinburgh: Edinburgh University Press.

Midgley, M. 2000 'The earthen long barrow phenomenon in Europe: creation of monumental cemeteries', in *In Memoriam Jan Rulf*, pp. 255–65, *Pamatky archeologické Supplementum* 13.

Miller, D. 1985 *Artefacts as Categories: a Study of Ceramic Variability in Central India*, Cambridge: Cambridge University Press.

Modderman, P. 1988 'The linear pottery culture. Diversity in unity', *Berichten van der Rijksdienst voor het Oudheidkundig Bodermonderzoek* 38: 63–139.

Mordant, C. 1998 'Emergence d'une architecture funéraire monumentale (vallées de la Seine et de l'Yonne)', in J. Guilaine (ed.), *Sépultures d'Occident et genèses des mégalithismes*, pp. 73–88, Paris: Errance.

Morris, I. 1986 'The use and abuse of Homer', *Classical Antiquity* 5(1): 81–138.

Müller, J. 1997 'Neolithische und chalkolithische Spondylus-Artefakte. Ammerkunden zu Verbreitung, Tauschgebiet und sozialer Funktion', in C. Becker (ed.), *Beitrage zur prähistorischen archäologie zwisches Nord- und Sudeuropa*, pp. 91–106, Espelkamp: Marie Leidorf.

Müller, J. 1999 'Zur Entstehung der Europäischen Megalithik', in K. Beinhauser, C. Guksch and S. Kus (eds), *Studien zur Megalithik. Forschunungestand und ethnoarchäologische Perspektiven*, pp. 51–81, Weissbach: Beier und Beran.

Newman, C. 1997 *Tara. An Archaeological Survey*, Dublin: The Discovery Programme.

Newman, C. 1999 'Astonishing new monument at Tara', *Past* 33: 1.

Olivier, L. 1999 'Duration, memory and the nature of the archaeological record', in A. Gustafsson and H. Karlsson (eds), *Glyfer och arkeologiska rum – ein vänbok till Jarl Nordbladh*, pp. 529–35, Gothenburg: Gotarc.

Ong, W. 1988 *Orality and Literacy. The Technologizing of the Word*, London: Routledge.

Parker Pearson, M. and Ramilisonina 1998 'Stonehenge for the ancestors: the stones pass on the message', *Antiquity* 72: 308–26.

Patton, M. 1993 *Statements in Stone. Monuments and Society in Neolithic Brittany*, London: Routledge.

Petrie, G. 1839 'On the history and antiquities of Tara Hill', *Transactions of the Royal Irish Academy* 18: 25–232.

Piggott, S. 1938 'The Early Bronze Age in Wessex', *Proceedings of the Prehistoric Society* 4: 52–106.

Piggott, S. 1989 *Ancient Britons and the Antiquarian Imagination*, London: Thames and Hudson.

Pinnigre, J.-F. 1990 'La nécropole de l'Age du Bronze de Conchil-le-Temple (Pas-de-Calais)', *Les Cahiers de Préhistoire du Nord* 8: 79–89.

Pitt Rivers, A. 1887–98 *Excavations in Cranborne Chase, Volumes 1–4*, privately published.

Pitts, M. 2001 'Excavating the Sanctuary: new investigations on Overton Hill, Avebury', *Wiltshire Archaeological Magazine* 94: 1–23.

Pollard, J. 1992 'The Sanctuary, Overton Hill: a re-examination', *Proceedings of the Prehistoric Society* 58: 213–26.

Price, T. D., Bentley, A., Lüning, J., Gronenborn, D. and Wahl, J. 2001 'Prehistoric human migration in the Linearbandkeramik of Central Europe', *Antiquity* 75: 593–603.

Pryor, F. 1998 *Etton: Excavations at a Neolithic Causewayed Enclosure Near Maxey, Cambridgeshire 1982–87*, London: English Heritage.

Pryor, F., French, C., Crowther, D., Gurney, D., Simpson, G. and Taylor, M. 1985 'Archaeology and environment in the Lower Welland Valley', *East Anglian Archaeology* 27.

Raftery, B. 1994 *Pagan Celtic Ireland*, London: Thames and Hudson.

Renfrew, C. 1998 'Mind and matter. Cognitive archaeology and external symbolic storage', in C. Renfrew and C. Scarre (eds), *Cognition and Material Culture: the Archaeology of Symbolic Storage*, pp. 1–6, Cambridge: McDonald Institute for Archaeological Research.

Rideout, J. 1997 'Excavation of a Neolithic enclosures at Cowie Road, Bannockburn, Stirling, 1984–5', *Proceedings of the Society of Antiquaries of Scotland* 127: 29–68.

Roche, H. 1999 'Late Iron Age activity at Tara, Co. Meath', *Ríocht na Midhe* 10: 18–30.

Sanches, M. J., Santos, P. M., Bradley, R. and Fábregas, R. 1998 'Land marks. a new approach to the rock art of Trás-os-Montes, Northern Portugal', *Journal of Iberian Archaeology* (1998): 85–104.

Scarre, C. 1992 'The Early Neolithic of Western France and megalithic origins in Atlantic Europe', *Oxford Journal of Archaeology* 11: 121–54.

Scarre, C. 1998 'Traditions of death, mounded tombs, megalithic art and funerary ideology in Neolithic Western Europe', in M. Edmonds and C. Richards (eds), *Understanding the Neolithic of North-western Europe*, pp. 161–87, Glasgow: Cruithne Press.

Scarre, C., Switsur, R. and Mohen, J. P. 1993 'New radiocarbon dates from Bougon and the chronology of French passage-graves', *Antiquity* 67: 856–9.

Sellier, D. 1995 'Elements de reconstitution du paysage prémégalithique sur le site des alignements de Kercado (Carnac, Morbihan) à partir les critères geomorphologiques', *Révue Archéologique de l'Ouest* 12: 21–44.

Shanks, M. and Tilley, C. 1987 *Social Theory and Archaeology*, Cambridge: Polity Press.

Shee Twohig, E. 1981 *The Megalithic Art of Western Europe*, Oxford: Clarendon Press.

Sherratt, A. 1990 'The genesis of megaliths: monumentality, ethnicity and social complexity in Neolithic north-west Europe', *World Archaeology* 22: 147–67.

Simonin, D. 1997 'Analyse spatiale d'un site d'habitat du Néolithique ancien à Echilleuse (Loiret)', in A. Bocquet (ed.), *Espaces physiques, espaces sociales dans l' analyse des sites du Néolithique à l'age du Fer*, pp. 345–68, Paris: Editions du CNRS.

Simpson, D. 1996 'Excavation of a kerbed funerary monument at Stoneyfield, Raigmore, Inverness, Highland 1972–3', *Proceedings of the Society of Antiquaries of Scotland* 126: 53–86.

Sisam, K. 1990 'Anglo-Saxon royal genealogies', in E. Stanley (ed.), *British Academy Papers on Anglo-Saxon England*, pp. 145–204, Oxford: Oxford University Press.

Sopp, M. 1999 *Die Wiederaufnahme älter Bestattungsplätze in den nachfolgenden vor- und frügeschichtlichen Perioden in Norddeutschland*, Bonn: Habelt.

Stäuble, H. and Lüning, J. 1999 'Phosphatanalysen in bandkeramischen Häusern', *Archäologisches Korrespondenzblatt* 29: 165–87.

Stead, I. 1991 *Iron Age Cemeteries in East Yorkshire*, London: English Heritage.

Stead, I. 1998 *The Salisbury Hoard*, Stroud: Tempus.

Stepanovic, M. 1997 'The age of clay. The social dynamics of house destruction', *Journal of Anthropological Archaeology* 16: 334–95.

Stoertz, C. 1997 *Ancient Landscapes of the Yorkshire Wolds*, Swindon: Royal Commission on the Historical Monuments of England.

Taylor, A. 1986 *The Welsh Castles of Edward I*, London: Hambledon Press.

Tempel, W. 1981 'Ein völkerwanderungzeitlicher Gräbhugel beim sächsischen Gräberfeld von Gudendorf, Stadt Cuxhaven, Niedersachsen', *Studien zur Sachsenforschung* 2: 447–55.

Therkorn, L. 1987 'The structures, mechanics and some aspects of inhabited behaviour', in R. Brandt, W. Groenman-van-Waateringe and S. van der Leeuw (eds), *Assendelver Polders Papers 1*, pp. 177–224, Amsterdam: Cingula 12.

Therkorn, L. and Abbink, A. 1987 'Some levée sites', in R. Brandt, W. Groenman-van-Waateringe and S. van der Leeuw (eds), *Assendelver Polders Papers 1*, pp. 115–67, Amsterdam: Cingula 12.

Thomas, J. 1996 *Time, Culture and Identity*, London: Routledge.

Thomas, J. 1999 *Understanding the Neolithic*, London: Routledge.

Thomas, J. 2000 'The identity of place in Neolithic Britain: examples from south-west Scotland', in A. Ritchie (ed.), *Neolithic Orkney in its European Context*, pp. 79–87, Cambridge: McDonald Institute for Archaeological Research.

Thompson, M. W. 1977 *General Pitt Rivers. Evolution and Archaeology in the Nineteenth Century*, Bradford on Avon: Moonraker Press.

Todd, M. 1987 *The South-West to AD 1000*, Harlow: Longman.

Trigger, B. 1980 'Archaeology and the image of the American Indian', *American Antiquity* 45: 662–76.

Trigger, B. 1989 *A History of Archaeological Thought*, Cambridge: Cambridge University Press.

Vandkilde, H. 1999 'Social distinction and ethnic reconstruction in the earliest Danish Bronze Age', in *Eliten in der Bronzezeit*, pp. 245–76, Mainz: Römisch-Germanische Zentralmuseum.

Vansina, J. 1985 *Oral Tradition as History*, Madison, WI: University of Wisconsin Press.

Veit, U. 1996 *Studien zur Problem der Siedlungbesattung in europäischen Neolithikum*, Mainz: Waxman.

Wailes, B. 1982 'The Irish "royal" sites in history and archaeology', *Cambridge Medieval Celtic Studies* 3: 1–29.

Wainwright, F. T. 1953 *The Problem of the Picts*, Edinburgh: Nelson.

Wainwright, G. and Smith, K. 1980 'The Shaugh Moor Project: second report – the enclosures', *Proceedings of the Prehistoric Society* 46: 65–122.

Wall, J. 1987 'The role of daggers in Early Bronze Age Britain: the evidence of wear analysis', *Oxford Journal of Archaeology* 6: 115–18.

Waterbolk, H. 1959 'Die bandkeramisches Siedlung von Geleen', *Palaeohistoria* 6–7: 132–67.

Waterbolk, H. 1961 'Bronzezeitlicher dreischiffinge Häuser von Elp', *Helinium* 1: 126–32.

Waterbolk, H. 1964 'The Bronze Age settlement of Elp', *Helinium* 4: 97–131.

Waterbolk, H. 1986 'Elp', in H. Beck, H. Jankuhn, K. Ranke and R. Wenksus (eds), *Reallexikon der Germanischen Altertunskunde* 7: 163–75, Berlin: De Gruyter.

Waterman, D. 1997 *Excavations at Navan Fort*, Belfast: Stationery Office.

Wesselinger, D. 2000 'Native neighbours. Local settlement systems and social structure in the Roman period at Oss (the Netherlands)', *Analecta Praehistorica Leidensia* 32.

Wheeler, R. E. M. 1954 *Archaeology from the Earth*, Oxford: Clarendon Press.

Whittle, A. 1996 *Europe in the Neolithic. The Creation of New Worlds*, Cambridge: Cambridge University Press.

Whittle, A. 2000 '"Very like a whale". Menhirs, motifs and myths in the Mesolithic–Neolithic transition of northwest Europe', *Cambridge Archaeological Journal* 10: 243–59.

Wilhelmi, K. 1990 'Ruinen und Nordhorn – zwischen Ijssel und Ems: besondere Rechteck- und Quadratgraben der Eisenzeit', *Helinium* 29: 92–122.

Williams, G. 1985 *When Was Wales?*, Harmondsworth: Penguin.

Woodbridge, K. 1970 *Landscape and Antiquity. Aspects of English Culture at Stourhead 1718 to 1838*, Oxford: Clarendon Press.

Woodward, A. 1999 'When did pots become domestic? Special pots and everyday pots in British prehistory', *Medieval Ceramics* 22–3: 3–10.

Woodward, A. 2000 'The prehistoric pottery', in G. Hughes (ed.), *The Lockington Gold Hoard*, pp. 48–61, Oxford: Oxbow.

Woodward, A. and Leach, P. 1993 *The Uley Shrines: Excavation of a Ritual Complex on West Hill, Uley, Gloucestershire*, London: English Heritage.

York, J. 2002 'The life cycle of Bronze Age metalwork from the Thames', *Oxford Journal of Archaeology* 21: 77–92.

Index